Business Meetings With God

A 90-DAY DEVOTIONAL FOR FAITH-BASED ENTREPRENEURS

TATUM TEMIA

For general information, visit the author's website at www.tatumtemia.com

Printed in the USA

ISBN-13: 9798500426727

Table of Contents

Introduction 5

Set Your Intentions. 6

New Goals, New Habits 10

Faith Check 12

Work Hard and in Excellence. . . . 14

Withholding Nothing 16

The Promises of God. 18

The Fruit of the Spirit 20

Heart Check. 22

Are You Proactive or Reactive?. . . 24

What Does the Word Say? 26

Problem Solver. 28

Ask and You Shall Receive 30

A Bigger Picture 32

The Road to Success 34

The Hype. 36

Here & Now 38

Live in Your Promises 40

Praise Him for All Things. 42

Examine the Promise 44

The Company You Keep
(Environment) 46

Play Both Sides. 48

History of Favor 50

Change Will Come 52

Grace & Forgiveness 54

Command Your Authority 56

The Spirit of God Fuels Your
Business 58

Praise the Most High 60

The Word Covers Your Life 62

Nothing Can Harm What God Has
Blessed 64

Focus on Freedom & Faith 66

Time for Skill and Poise. 68

Abandon Your Fear 70

Power Within Your Flaws 72

Respect God's Time 74

A Basket Filled with Faithful Prayer
Will Bring Much 76

Pulled from Doom to Glory 78

Dreams Tied to Realities 80

Never Mind What Others
Are Doing 82

Light Up Your Journey 84

Look Forward to Your Harvest . . . 86

Always Be the Best You Can Be. . . 88

Use It and Don't Lose It 90

Wins From Losses. 92

Heart Check Part 2 94

Your Flesh Is Not A Leader. 96

Business Meeting Notes 97

Time With God. 98

The Ten Percent Perspective

Shift 100

Strong Enough to Power You . . . 102

Valued Relationships. 104

Your Build-Up to

Prominence 106

Stand by Your Creator. 108

Serve to Surpass. 110

Mind Your Development 112

Make God's Wisdom A Thing 114

You Shall Be Comforted. 116

Alone Yet Unafraid 118

Serve as God's Prize 120

Unfathomable Favor 122

Let Your Gifts Shine 124

He Works in Strange Ways. 126

Be Mindful of the Fruits of

Your Labor. 128

Grace-Filled Experience 130

Wait On Him 132

Never For the Love of Money . . . 134

Take Your Lessons to Heart 136

Let Wisdom Be Your Guide. 138

Trusting in You 140

Answer the Call Without

Ceasing 142

He That Builds You Up 144

Reminder to Shape Your

Perspective 146

Consuming Spirit 148

Practice Makes Perfect 150

Unpacking Visions 152

Keep Anxiety Out 154

Not Too Fast, But Not Too Slow. . 156

Health Is Wealth. 158

A Calling Above Man 160

Confidence in Your Calling 162

What Will They Call You? 164

Hallelujah 166

Faith in the Unseen. 168

Eat to Live 170

Like Music for the Soul 172

Fruit from the Tree of

Fulfillment. 174

The Gift of Ability. 176

All Things New 178

Fasting God's Way. 180

Preparation Mindset. 182

Assets > Liabilities 184

New Beginnings 186

Author Bio. 189

Introduction

Welcome to *Business Meetings with God: A 90-Day Devotional for Faith Based Entrepreneurs*. This is not your average devotional. Instead it's a space that helps you connect your role as an entrepreneur with your role as a child of God, once and for all. For too long we've been programmed to believe faith and business should stay separated in our lives. However, God didn't place ideas, ministries, products, or services within us to be executed without His direction. By consistently seeking Him first, you align yourself and your business with His divine assignment for your life.

The concept of a business meeting with God is for you to put into practice seeking Him on behalf of your business. When I have a business meeting with God, I go in with open ended questions, a notebook to write in, and sometimes even a white board to draw out all of the things He reveals to me. It's not a space where you go and tell God all of your ideas and ask Him to bless them. Rather, a space you enter as the manager that is implementing His divine plan. Business meetings with God are a space for you to humble yourself and realize that no matter what title you hold on paper, He is indeed the CEO and the ultimate strategist. It is then your job to leave that meeting and apply what He revealed.

Think about this…after we're born, our identity is shaped largely by factors and experiences that oftentimes have nothing to do with God. It is unfortunate that we can grow apart from Him but this devotional bridges that gap. Through 90 days of consistently seeking God on behalf of your business, you will see a definite shift in your life. You will begin to experience a peace that surpasses all understanding. *"The Lord your God will then make you successful in everything you do. He will give you many children and numerous livestock, and He will cause your fields to produce abundant harvests, for the LORD will again delight in being good to you as He was to your ancestors." - Deuteronomy 15:10*

Enjoy!

XO,
TATUM

Set Your Intentions

The business world will tell you a host of things you need to do at the start of the quarter. That may include reviewing accounting information from previous quarters, analyzing the progress of goals set in the beginning of the year, projecting sales for the quarter, etc. All of those are wise for any entrepreneur or business owner to keep up with. However, as a believer and with God as your CEO, success for this quarter is more than what your projections, balance sheet, or profit and loss statements tell you.

The success of your character and the progress you make towards God's plan for your life is a top priority. Set your intentions for the quarter by taking into account more than just the business. Measure how obedient you have been up until today. Have you done everything God has told you to do? Has your prayer life been consistent? Do you know God more intimately this quarter than you did in prior quarters? As you enter into the next 90-days, set your intentions for your spiritual life, just as you do your business life. Success is not about how much money you can make, how many clients you have, or how many products you sell. Success is solely pleasing God and He will give you all of the desires in your heart. In your meeting with Him this morning, ask Him to show you what He needs from you this quarter. Ask Him to reveal the areas within you and your business that He needs for you to improve. Make your goals for the next 90-days, His goals.

Then the Lord replied: "Write the vision and make it plain on tablets, That he may run who reads it. For the vision is yet for an appointed time; But at the end it will speak, and it will not lie. Though it tarries, wait for it; Because it will surely come, It will not tarry.
HABAKKUK 2:2-3 (NIV)

But if you remain in me and my words remain in you, you may ask for anything you want, and it will be granted!
JOHN 15:7 (NLT)

God Goals

_____
_____
_____
_____
_____
_____
_____
_____
_____
_____
_____
_____
_____
_____
_____
_____
_____
_____
_____
_____
_____

DATE: _____ / ____ / _____

God Goals

_____

_____

_____

_____

_____

_____

_____

_____

_____

_____

_____

_____

_____

_____

_____

_____

_____

_____

_____

_____

God Goals

_____

_____

_____

_____

_____

_____

_____

_____

_____

_____

_____

_____

_____

_____

_____

_____

_____

_____

_____

New Goals, New Habits

As you do the things of God, you must also work to be an example of Christ in the business world. As humans, we are imperfect and will always make mistakes but our intentions should be to exude the same love and respect that Jesus did when he was on the earth. We may be short-tempered and quick to react emotionally, but the bible tells us that we are to control our emotions.

You've experienced a time you were wronged by someone and wanted to cut them off, but God says to love them and pray for them. We may get frustrated when our circumstances don't reflect what God said, but the Bible tells us we are to walk by faith and not by sight. It's time to level up in the kingdom which will also reflect positively in your entrepreneurial life. If you strive to be like Christ, you can handle a rude or disrespectful customer with tact. When someone attacks your character, you will be able to pray for them without being offended and without any urge to reciprocate negatively.

As you grow in influence and affluence, your increased responsibility should not increase your anxiety, but rather increase your dependence on God. Surrendering to God means dying to yourself every day so that you can do His will and not your own. As you meet with God this morning, ask Him which habits you need to change in order to be more like Him. Ask Him which tests you've been failing that are necessary to handle the next level He has for you. Write down the answers He gives you and commit to being more like Christ every day.

This means that anyone who belongs to Christ has become a new person. The old life is gone; a new life has begun!
2 CORINTHIANS 5:17 (NLT)

Those who say they live in God should live their lives as Jesus did.
1 JOHN 2:6 (NLT)

Business Meeting Notes

DATE: _____ / / _____

_____

_____

_____

_____

_____

_____

_____

_____

_____

_____

_____

_____

_____

_____

_____

_____

_____

_____

_____

_____

_____

_____

Faith Check

How is your faith in God as your CEO? Be honest. Have you been worrying about "how"? Have you been stressing over the outcome of things you're working on? Have you been anxious about where God's promises to you are going to come from? If so, you have little faith. The scripture above says, God made the earth out of nothing that could be seen. The bible also says that God can do infinitely above anything we can ask or imagine.

As a believer, what makes you think you can figure God out? You're stressed because you're making yourself anxious and not resting in what God said. Sometimes the enemy doesn't have to attack externally. All he has to do is make you worry. Your worrying causes you to take back what you've previously surrendered to God and also causes you to make the mistake of thinking you can do better than the Lord.

Stop looking at the scoreboard and play the game. When you are in alignment with God the game is rigged in your favor anyway. Busy yourself with obedience and don't waste time worrying about the result. In your meeting with God this morning, ask Him to check your faith. Ask Him to reveal to you what's holding you back from fully trusting in His plan and what you need to do to change it. Add whatever He tells you to your to-do list for the day.

Faith shows the reality of what we hope for; it is the evidence of things we cannot see. Through their faith, people in the days of old earned a good reputation. By faith we understand that the entire universe was formed at God's command, that what we now see did not come from anything that can be seen. It was by faith that Abel brought a more acceptable offering to God than Cain did. Abel's offering gave evidence that he was a righteous man, and God showed his approval of his gifts. Although Abel is long dead, he still speaks to us by his example of faith. It was by faith that Enoch was taken up to heaven without dying—"he disappeared, because God took him." For before he was taken up, he was known as a person who pleased God. And it is impossible to please God without faith. Anyone who wants to come to Him must believe that God exists and that He rewards those who sincerely seek Him.
HEBREWS 11:1-6 (NLT)

Business Meeting Notes

DATE: _____ / / _____

_____
_____
_____
_____
_____
_____
_____
_____
_____
_____
_____
_____
_____
_____
_____
_____
_____
_____
_____
_____
_____
_____
_____

Work Hard and in Excellence

The Bible says that faith without works is dead. In the previous entry, we assessed the quality of faith and today we will assess the quality of work you add alongside your faith. Success is guaranteed when business is done God's way, but we must still work hard and work in excellence.

Excellence is defined as the quality of being outstanding or extremely good. God is an excellent God! We, ourselves, must be excellent in all we do as well. Using the above definition, has your work been excellent so far in this quarter? Are you being productive and effective or are you just busy? Have you done your absolute best and left no stone unturned? Have you maximized your time each day? Have you truly sat in God's presence each day or just rushed through it? If you were your customer, what would your opinion be of your business? As you sit with God this morning, ask Him if He is satisfied with the quality of work. Ask Him to reveal to you what you need to do today to be more excellent.

What good is it, my brothers and sisters, if someone claims to have faith but has no deeds? Can such faith save them? Suppose a brother or a sister is without clothes and daily food. If one of you says to them, "Go in peace; keep warm and well fed," but does nothing about their physical needs, what good is it? In the same way, faith by itself, if it is not accompanied by action is dead.
JAMES 2:14–17 (NIV)

66

SUCCESS IS GUARANTEED WHEN BUSINESS IS DONE GOD'S WAY, BUT WE MUST STILL WORK HARD AND WORK IN EXCELLENCE.

99

Business Meeting Notes

DATE: _____ / / _____

_____

_____

_____

_____

_____

_____

_____

_____

_____

_____

_____

_____

_____

_____

_____

_____

_____

_____

_____

_____

_____

_____

_____

_____

_____

Withholding Nothing

I often used the phrase, *"Broken people build broken businesses."* In today's world, brokenness is a norm—so much so that we don't know where to begin our healing. We all have things about us that we aren't proud about. We've buried certain memories from our past in hopes of never revisiting those experiences again. We may be able to avoid our own feelings, but we should never put up a guard with God. He is all-knowing and He wants us to surrender even those secret places to Him. Those secret places tend to resurface in our businesses, even when we don't realize it. For example, 'daddy issues' can become trust issues with potential business affiliates who God may have sent us. We have been hurt by friends before, so because we don't let anyone close to us, we miss out on the covenant relationships God sent to cover and pray for us on our journey. We were bullied growing up, so as soon as someone leaves a negative comment on a social media page, we feel that we must respond to defend ourselves.

Just because we have learned to cope with our brokenness doesn't make our healing less important. God wants us to surrender everything to Him so that He can make you successful in business and in life. Are there things you have been too ashamed to bring up to God? Are there memories you would rather forget than to pray about? Are there people you still need to forgive? Talk to God about it in your meeting this morning and ask Him how these things are affecting your business.

Trust in the Lord with all your heart and lean not on your own understanding; in all your ways submit to Him, and He will make your paths straight.
PROVERBS 3:5-6 (NIV)

Then He said to the crowd, "If any of you wants to be my follower, you must give up your own way, take up your cross daily, and follow me. If you try to hang on to your life, you will lose it. But if you give up your life for my sake, you will save it.
LUKE 9:23-24 (NLT)

Business Meeting Notes

DAY 5

DATE: _____ / ____ / _____

_____
_____
_____
_____
_____
_____
_____
_____
_____
_____
_____
_____
_____
_____
_____
_____
_____
_____
_____
_____
_____
_____
_____

The Promises of God

Control is a natural desire for us as a human race even if we know God's way is better. Taking action into our own hands can provide a sense of comfort. However, we have to tame that desire for control over our business as we accept that our business belongs to God and we humbly serve in a management role. Before you meet with Him this morning, reflect on more of His promises and take comfort in trusting Him.

And my God will meet all your needs according to the riches of His glory in Christ Jesus.
PHILIPPIANS 4:19 (NIV)

The Lord himself will fight for you. Just stay calm.
EXODUS 14:14 (NLT)

Remember the Lord your God. He is the one who gives you power to be successful, in order to fulfill the covenant he confirmed to your ancestors with an oath.
DEUTERONOMY 8:18 (NLT)

Don't be afraid, for I am with you. Don't be discouraged, for I am your God. I will strengthen you and help you. I will hold you up with my victorious right hand.
ISAIAH 41:10 (NLT)

When you go through deep waters, I will be with you. When you go through rivers of difficulty, you will not drown. When you walk through the fire of oppression, you will not be burned up; the flames will not consume you.
ISAIAH 43:2 (NLT)

Additional Scriptures:

But in that coming day no weapon turned against you will succeed. You will silence every voice raised up to accuse you. These benefits are enjoyed by the servants of the Lord; their vindication will come from me. I, the Lord, have spoken!
ISAIAH 54:17 (NLT)

"For I know the plans I have for you," says the Lord. "They are plans for good and not for disaster, to give you a future and a hope.
JEREMIAH 29:11 (NLT)

"I knew you before I formed you in your mother's womb. Before you were born I set you apart and appointed you as my prophet to the nations."
JEREMIAH 1:5 (NLT)

I tell you, you can pray for anything, and if you believe that you've received it, it will be yours.
MARK 11:24 (NLT)

Business Meeting Notes

DATE: _____ / / _____

_____

_____

_____

_____

_____

_____

_____

_____

_____

_____

_____

_____

_____

_____

_____

_____

_____

_____

_____

_____

_____

_____

The Fruit of the Spirit

The fruit of the Spirit is the measuring stick for us to know if we are walking in one accord with the Holy Spirit. If you find yourself lacking love, peace, forbearance, kindness, goodness, faithfulness, gentleness, or self-control then it is time to reconnect with God. Draw closer to Him and ask Him to replenish whatever you are lacking.

In entrepreneurship, it is easy to step out of line with the Holy Spirit. A business deal can go wrong and steal your joy or a sale can take too long and steal your peace. It is natural for our emotions to fluctuate, but you must always be intentional in regaining alignment with God. When God is your CEO, you don't operate in the natural, you operate in the Spirit. You must constantly remind your flesh in the midst of any storm, you will always have joy and peace because the Lord promised it to you. Do you find yourself lacking in any of the fruit of the spirit? In your meeting with God this morning, ask Him what's required of you to get back in step with the Spirit.

But the fruit of the Spirit is love, joy, peace, forbearance, kindness, goodness, faithfulness, gentleness and self-control. Against such things there is no law. Those who belong to Christ Jesus have crucified the flesh with its passions and desires. Since we live by the Spirit, let us keep in step with the Spirit. Let us not become conceited, provoking and envying each other.
GALATIANS 5:22-26 (NIV)

DRAW CLOSER TO HIM AND ASK HIM TO REPLENISH WHATEVER YOU ARE LACKING.

Business Meeting Notes

DATE: _____ / ___ / _____

Heart Check

Are you truly seeking God with your whole heart or are you harboring skepticism, trying to figure Him out and anticipate His next move? If God made the heavens and the earth from absolutely nothing what makes you think that you can figure Him out?

God wants you to be as passionate about Him as you are about your business. You research everything as it relates to business. You're reading all the top business books and following your favorite success stories on Instagram because in your heart of hearts you yearn to be successful. God wants that type of passion towards pleasing Him. In fact, He wants you to desire pleasing Him more than you desire to be successful. In Genesis, the story of Abraham describes the years and decades it took to have a son. Abraham was so passionate and excited about having a son—similar to how you are about your business. One day, God told him to sacrifice his son; this very son he'd been waiting for his entire life to receive. Nevertheless, he was obedient and just as he prepared to sacrifice his son, God stopped him. He saw that Abraham's heart was in the right place and as a result of the observed obedience all of Abraham's descendants were blessed.

Are you willing to sacrifice your goals for God? In your meeting this morning, ask God if there's anything you've been putting ahead of Him that you didn't realize.

Jesus replied, "You must love the Lord your God with all your heart, all your soul, and all your mind."
MATTHEW 22:37 (NLT)

"Yes, I am the vine; you are the branches. Those who remain in me, and I in them, will produce much fruit. For apart from me you can do nothing."
JOHN 15:5 (NLT)

I say then: Walk in the Spirit, and you shall not fulfill the lust of the flesh. For the flesh lusts against the Spirit, and the Spirit against the flesh; and these are contrary to one another, so that you do not do the things that you wish. But if you are led by the Spirit, you are not under the law.
GALATIANS 5:16-18 (NKJV)

Business Meeting Notes

DAY
8

DATE: _____ / / _____

_____

_____

_____

_____

_____

_____

_____

_____

_____

_____

_____

_____

_____

_____

_____

_____

_____

_____

_____

_____

_____

_____

Are You Proactive or Reactive?

We discussed in a prior entry how many of us get into a habit of only praying from a defensive stance. When we get sick, we pray. When something bad happens in our lives, we pray. When our finances take a hit, we pray. When our customer and clientele numbers are dropping, we pray. When was the last time you prayed some things into existence? When was the last time you hopped on the offensive line in your prayer life? The Bible says that you will declare a thing and it will be established.

Today in your time with God, write out a list of declarations. Be sure that your list is aligned with God's word and the plan He has for your life.

You will also declare a thing, And it will be established for you; So light will shine on your ways.
JOB 22:28 (NKJV)

"

WHEN WAS THE LAST TIME YOU HOPPED ON THE OFFENSIVE LINE IN YOUR PRAYER LIFE?

"

Business Meeting Notes

DATE: ___/___/___

_____

_____

_____

_____

_____

_____

_____

_____

_____

_____

_____

_____

_____

_____

_____

_____

_____

_____

_____

_____

_____

What Does the Word Say?

This may sound silly, but I didn't know the Bible had so much wisdom for everyday life until I began to study it for myself. Many of us make the mistake of having second-hand faith. We rely on inspirational pages, pastors, and books to tell us what God said. The danger from constantly relying on third parties is gullible and susceptible to being taught the wrong thing.

By meditating on the Word for yourself, you are able to internalize what God said. Eventually, you will see His promises come to pass in your life and business. When was the last time you dove into a scripture or a Biblical story? Have you been reading the Word daily? Add that to your to-do list for today. In your time with God, ask Him to lead you to a scripture that speaks to what He wants to do in your life and business. Meditate on it day and night.

Study this Book of Instruction continually. Meditate on it day and night so you will be sure to obey everything written in it. Only then will you prosper and succeed in all you do.
JOSHUA 1:8 (NLT)

> **BY MEDITATING ON THE WORD FOR YOURSELF, YOU ARE ABLE TO INTERNALIZE WHAT GOD SAID.**

Business Meeting Notes

DATE: ___ / / ___

_____

_____

_____

_____

_____

_____

_____

_____

_____

_____

_____

_____

_____

_____

_____

_____

_____

_____

_____

_____

_____

_____

Problem Solver

Are you struggling to find a strategy to implement in your business? No need to worry because you aren't the first and you won't be the last. This won't prevent you from taking your side-hustle to a full-time occupation. The ability to solve problems is what gives entrepreneurs their platform. God tells us that if we struggle with anything, we can ask for wisdom and He will give it to us. The only catch is that we can't doubt the answers we receive.

Anytime we surrender to a problem we contribute to the actual problem. The core of entrepreneurship is to provide valuable solutions. Whenever you have a problem that comes up in your business, your job is to solve it and not magnify the problem. Instead of allowing issues to block your progress, trust God to lead you to what you can do to solve it and have faith that you can accomplish the task.

If any of you lacks wisdom, you should ask God, who gives generously to all without finding fault, and it will be given to you. But when you ask, you must believe and not doubt, because the one who doubts is like a wave of the sea, blown and tossed by the wind.
JAMES 1:5-6 (NIV)

GOD TELLS US THAT IF WE STRUGGLE
WITH ANYTHING, WE CAN ASK FOR
WISDOM AND HE WILL GIVE IT TO US.

Business Meeting Notes

DATE: _____ / / _____

_____

_____

_____

_____

_____

_____

_____

_____

_____

_____

_____

_____

_____

_____

_____

_____

_____

_____

_____

_____

_____

_____

Ask and You Shall Receive

Many times we allow the specific wording of our prayer requests to hinder us from recognizing when they have been answered. For example, when we ask God for financial increase we expect to somehow receive a random check. If that doesn't happen, we feel that our prayers went unanswered and our faith takes a hit. In reality, God has given us everything we need for our requests to come together. He gave us all the ingredients for the recipe, but if we allow our limited perspective to blind us, we easily miss the pieces of the puzzle which are within our reach.

Jesus tells us in the scripture that when we approach God in prayer, we shall not be disappointed. We should exercise patience and should be reflective on our situation. Because of God's persistent work in our lives, we can do all things and we lack nothing. As we open up our hearts and minds to God, we will not fail to see how He has truly blessed us. Ask God to shift your focus today so that your eyes can be opened to the realities of His goodness.

Ask and it will be given to you; seek and you will find; knock and the door will be opened to you. For everyone who asks receives; the one who seeks finds; and to the one who knocks, the door will be opened.
MATTHEW 7:7-8 (NIV)

The Lord will guide you always; He will satisfy your needs in a sun-scorched land and will strengthen your frame. You will be like a well-watered garden, like a spring whose waters never fail.
ISAIAH 58:11 (NIV)

> ❝
> BECAUSE OF GOD'S PERSISTENT WORK IN OUR LIVES, WE CAN DO ALL THINGS AND WE LACK NOTHING.
> ❞

Business Meeting Notes

DATE: _____/____/_____

_____
_____
_____
_____
_____
_____
_____
_____
_____
_____
_____
_____
_____
_____
_____
_____
_____
_____
_____
_____
_____
_____
_____
_____

A Bigger Picture

There are several reasons why chasing after God and what He wants for you is non-negotiable. In the scripture, Joseph explained to his very own brothers that they shouldn't be angry for plotting to kill him nor for selling him to Egypt. He forgave them because of his faith. He suffered prison-time for mistaken identity and held on to his faith while giving God the credit for the gifts of interpreting dreams. He credited God for eventually placing him in a position to help those in need while all the land suffered severe famine.

As Joseph realized the bigger picture, think of what disobedience would mean for the people around you? If you decide not to repair relationships that you have, how would that impact your legacy? How would that affect your future? Don't get so caught up in the fear of being led by your faith that you abandon your faithwalk. Ask yourself "What if I don't?". What will that mean for the person, or people, that God wants you to help? You are a beacon of hope for somebody. If you surrender to your battles, what does that mean for them? Don't sacrifice the establishment of your legacy for temporary concerns over bills and disagreements. God has given you so much more!

God has sent me ahead of you to keep you and your families alive and to preserve many survivors. So it was God who sent me here...
GENESIS 45:7-8 (NLT)

> ## DON'T GET SO CAUGHT UP IN THE FEAR OF BEING LED BY YOUR FAITH THAT YOU ABANDON YOUR FAITHWALK.

Business Meeting Notes

DATE: ___ / / ___

_____
_____
_____
_____
_____
_____
_____
_____
_____
_____
_____
_____
_____
_____
_____
_____
_____
_____
_____
_____
_____

The Road to Success

Don't run away from growth! Too many people get so fixated on instant success that they disregard the real and painful process it takes to achieve true success. Personal development is as important, if not more important than business development. While it can be difficult, your overall quality of life improves as a result. Through personal development you enable yourself to be a better leader, influencer, or entrepreneur. You become a better servant of God, and of people.

Don't allow yourself to be swept in the hype when people advertise their overnight success stories. God wants us to become wholesome people who can eventually grow from our brokenness. Abiding by God's will and growing in it does not exempt you from struggles along your path. However it does **GUARANTEE** success that will endure throughout your life! The discipline, the instructions, and the lessons you learn in your growth process will stay with you and keep you on track as long as you live.

Enter through the narrow gate. For wide is the gate and broad is the road that leads to destruction, and many enter through it. But small is the gate and narrow the road that leads to life, and only a few find it.
MATTHEW 7:13-14 (NIV)

66

GOD WANTS US TO BECOME WHOLESOME
PEOPLE WHO CAN EVENTUALLY GROW FROM
OUR BROKENNESS.

99

Business Meeting Notes

DATE: ___/___/___

_____

_____

_____

_____

_____

_____

_____

_____

_____

_____

_____

_____

_____

_____

_____

_____

_____

_____

_____

_____

_____

_____

_____

The Hype

The bible tells us to worship Him and to love one another as we love ourselves. Loving your neighbor does not mean worshipping your neighbor. We can become so enthusiastic about influencers and our role models that we idolize the ground they walk on. If this is you, first you have to realize that you are no different from your role model. They were made in God's likeness just as you were. Never shrink yourself and place other people on a pedestal. We want to avoid such behavior and run to God instead. The only one that you need to exalt in any way is God who deserves all the glory! Although we can't see Him, it is important that we position ourselves under God to intentionally hear from Him.

The bible tells us to seek wise counsel. If the Holy Spirit leads you to seek wise counsel after prayer time, follow His guidance and be sure to take time to assess their qualifications to assist you. True helpers from your camp will emerge.

That you may be children of your father in heaven. He causes His sun to rise on the evil and the good, and sends rain on the righteous and the unrighteous.
MATTHEW 5:45 (NIV)

Plans fail for lack of counsel, but with many advisers they succeed.
PROVERBS 15:22 (NIV)

NEVER SHRINK YOURSELF AND PLACE OTHER PEOPLE ON A PEDESTAL.

Business Meeting Notes

DATE: _____ / / _____

_____

_____

_____

_____

_____

_____

_____

_____

_____

_____

_____

_____

_____

_____

_____

_____

_____

_____

_____

_____

_____

_____

Here & Now

Take time to be thankful about what God is doing for you right now. It's easy to focus on what's next - it's easy to get lost in worrying about when God will answer your prayers. Your urgency will make you forget to bask in appreciation for what He's done as of today and right now. What is taking you away from that?

God has given you dominion since birth and it is for you to exercise. Anxiety is the opposite of dominion. Anxiety is accompanied by stress, which stealthily creeps into your life while you constantly focus on what's next. You can find yourself being anxious over the same few things for years and years. Succumbing to this revolving fear is similar to the behavior of a hamster on a wheel. Remove yourself from the hamster wheel and exercise your dominion today! If God tells you something, have peace about it because whatever He promises will happen. Do yourself the favor of living stress free with God by your side.

So don't worry about tomorrow, for tomorrow will bring its own worries.
Today's trouble is enough for today.
MATTHEW 6:34 (NLT)

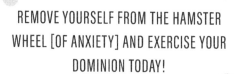

REMOVE YOURSELF FROM THE HAMSTER WHEEL [OF ANXIETY] AND EXERCISE YOUR DOMINION TODAY!

Business Meeting Notes

DATE: _____/____/_____

_____
_____
_____
_____
_____
_____
_____
_____
_____
_____
_____
_____
_____
_____
_____
_____
_____
_____
_____
_____
_____
_____
_____

Live in Your Promises

What do you envision in life and where do you see yourself over the next few years? Are you believing in God's promises and waiting on Him? Because of your faith, God will allow you to live above your physical means and live according to those promises. Faith is believing what God said is going to be true. The book of revelations makes several appeals for believers to be persistent in their faith as God performs His works. It is revealed to us that God fulfills His promises to create a paradise for us that is free from the concerns we may face today.

Take shelter in the promises He spoke to you. But how? How can you live in that space of what God said while you still operate based on what you see? One practical answer is to journal—write down your prayers and the things that God tells you. Write down the promises God has for you and look at them at the start of your day. Revisit the promises multiple times during the day—each time increasing the strength in your faith. Take a moment to reflect on the promises when you review them. It's not always about what you see around you but more about living in anticipation of what God will bring.

This calls for patient endurance on the part of the people of God who keep His commands and remain faithful to Jesus.
REVELATIONS 14:12 (NIV)

66

FAITH IS BELIEVING WHAT GOD SAID IS GOING TO BE TRUE.

99

Business Meeting Notes

DATE: _____ / / _____

_____

_____

_____

_____

_____

_____

_____

_____

_____

_____

_____

_____

_____

_____

_____

_____

_____

_____

_____

_____

_____

_____

_____

_____

Praise Him for All Things

In your environment, allow yourself to be gracious and appreciative and to freely worship God. Carry praise and worship with you wherever you go. Praise Him continuously for what He has always done and for what He continues to do in your life! The scripture above shows how a song of praise helped to free prisoners through supernatural means.

As a result of your praise, your overall appearance changes. It changes the look on your face and the mood you're in. Listen to worship music and talk to God on your commute AND free time. The Spirit of God has a way of forcing you to feel triumphant before whomever you interact. The Holy Spirit transforms and renews you from within. A song of praise in your heart will make you more appreciative of what's going on as God continues to perform His works.

Let the word of Christ dwell in you richly in all wisdom, teaching and admonishing one another in psalms and hymns and spiritual songs, singing with grace in your hearts to the Lord.
COLOSSIANS 3:16-17 (NKJV)

Around midnight Paul and Silas were praying and singing hymns to God, and other prisoners were listening. Suddenly, there was a massive earthquake, and the prison was shaken to its foundations. All the doors immediately flew open, and the chains of every prisoner fell off!
ACTS 16:25-26 (NIV)

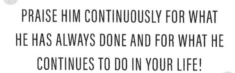

PRAISE HIM CONTINUOUSLY FOR WHAT HE HAS ALWAYS DONE AND FOR WHAT HE CONTINUES TO DO IN YOUR LIFE!

Business Meeting Notes

DATE: _____/____/_____

Examine the Promise

God is jealous about your love for Him. He wants you to seek Him at every point in your journey. Allow yourself to be influenced by God's word through prayer. Although it may seem repetitive to say but, dive in and spend uninterrupted time learning about the things God promised you. It's your duty to infuse the things of God into your life so that it resembles what He designed on your behalf.

With this in mind, ask yourself a real question—is social media helping your growth or deterring it? What kinds of things hold your attention on social media? Consider adjusting your usage to enhance your focus on the things of God. Make changes to the types of content you consume and expose yourself to things that reflect the Lord's promises. Make more room for God's promises to magnify them in your environment. Are your feeds consuming your time or helping you to better manage your time? Do they lead you to praise God and build your business according to His will? Is the content leading you to solve problems? Let God lead you to your rightful position in life and be sure to eliminate distractions that keep you off your journey.

Be careful not to forget the covenant of the Lord your God that He made with you; do not make for yourselves an idol in the form of anything the Lord your God has forbidden. For the Lord your God is a consuming fire, a jealous God.
DEUTERONOMY 4:23-24 (NIV)

Finally, brothers and sisters, whatever is true, whatever is noble, whatever is right, whatever is pure, whatever is lovely, whatever is admirable—if anything is excellent or praiseworthy—think about such things.
PHILIPPIANS 4:8 (NIV)

Business Meeting Notes

DATE: _____ / / _____

_____
_____
_____
_____
_____
_____
_____
_____
_____
_____
_____
_____
_____
_____
_____
_____
_____
_____
_____
_____
_____
_____

The Company You Keep
(Environment)

Healthy friendships and relationships reinforce the pursuit of the promises God has for you. Good friends sharpen you and keep you vigilant on your journey. Even if you don't have the most ideal friendships at the moment, pray for God to establish the relationships He knows you need in your life. Pray that He sends people who understand your faith walk and your strive toward progress. It is extremely difficult to handle everything you may be experiencing on your own.

Pray that He puts you in the right places at the right times to form these relationships. He will always place people in our lives that will give us signs and confirmations when we need them. These same individuals will sharpen our vision and also provide words and insight to help us further understand our calling. They will vouch for us as we enter new territory. They will offer useful resources that assist our climb. It is ultimately up to us to take heed when we're approached by people He sent to us. Are there individuals in your life that you need to contact? Has anyone come into your life that could be a messenger or a worker of God? Grow your network and make them welcome in your company.

Walk with the wise and become wise, for a companion of fools suffers harm.
PROVERBS 13:20 (NIV)

Now there was a certain disciple at Damascus named Ananias; and to him the Lord said in a vision, "Ananias." And he said, "Here I am Lord." So the Lord said to him, "Arise and go to the street called Straight, and inquire at the house of Judas for one called Saul of Tarsus, for behold, he is praying. And in a vision he has seen a man named Ananias coming in and putting his hand on him, so that he might receive his sight."
ACTS 9:10-12 (NKJV)

Business Meeting Notes

DATE: _____ / _____ / _____

_____

_____

_____

_____

_____

_____

_____

_____

_____

_____

_____

_____

_____

_____

_____

_____

_____

_____

_____

_____

_____

_____

Play Both Sides

Part of learning to fight spiritually is understanding that fighting is about offense as well as defense. The Lord is our strength as well as our defender and He equips us with the power of words as a way to profess our faith and to declare favor over our lives. Don't sit back and wait for things to happen before taking action! For example, don't wait to become sick before you begin a healing prayer for you or those close to you. Rather, declare with your mouth that you are healed when you're not experiencing any illness. Proactively speak the Word on your life before anything even happens. Recall that faith requires you to operate in the unseen as if it were already true.

At some point in your life, you've realized that it is never wise to wait for things to happen to you. As you take an aggressive position, seek God for guidance. Let Him inspire you to follow His lead. Commit to being obedient to what He says to you so that you closely align yourself with the path He has carved for you. With your words, cast away any stumbling blocks keeping you from that path which is free from harm and despair and filled with peace and mercy.

A man's stomach will be satisfied with the fruit of his mouth; He will be satisfied with the consequences of his words. Death and life are in the power of the tongue, and those who love it and indulge it will eat its fruit and bear the consequences of their words.
PROVERBS 18:20-21 (AMP)

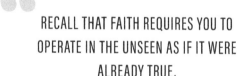

RECALL THAT FAITH REQUIRES YOU TO OPERATE IN THE UNSEEN AS IF IT WERE ALREADY TRUE.

Business Meeting Notes

DATE: _____/____/_____

_____
_____
_____
_____
_____
_____
_____
_____
_____
_____
_____
_____
_____
_____
_____
_____
_____
_____
_____
_____
_____
_____

History of Favor

How do you build the muscle to trust God more? Would you say you trust God in all things? It's very possible for some of us to have trust issues with people in our lives. However, be mindful not to allow your relationship with God to be impacted. God performs exceedingly and abundantly over our expectations so we should avoid treating that Godly relationship the same way we treat our relationships with friends, family, and acquaintances.

The way to build the muscle to trust God is to take inventory on answered prayers. By tracking and documenting the things God has done for you, you'll quickly identify His proven track record with you. You recall situations when He protected you when you were vulnerable. He carried you through tough times when you were immature and didn't understand the consequences of your behavior. He provided at a time when you thought it to be impossible. The list of blessings goes on and on.

Seeing it for yourself in this very manner encourages you to continue doing what God tells you. If He brought you this far, imagine how much more you will see if you continue to trust in His guidance and direction. It's written in the scripture that He is here for you.

Now this is the confidence that we have in Him, that if we ask anything according to His will, He hears us. And if we know that He hears us, whatever we ask, we know that we have the petitions that we have asked of Him.
1 JOHN 5:14-15 (NKJV)

66

THE WAY TO BUILD THE MUSCLE TO TRUST GOD IS TO TAKE INVENTORY ON ANSWERED PRAYERS.

99

Business Meeting Notes

DATE: _____ / / _____

_____

_____

_____

_____

_____

_____

_____

_____

_____

_____

_____

_____

_____

_____

_____

_____

_____

_____

_____

_____

_____

_____

_____

Change Will Come

How do you fight your battles? One way you can choose to fight is through prayer and fasting. On this very day, are you expecting something in life that does not seem to be taking form as you had hoped? Internal battles such as this should be fought through fasting and prayer. Not only is it recommended against your expectations but also for external challenges you're facing as well.

Turn down your plate, go deeper into the Word of God—things change. If it's still relatively early in your growing relationship with God you might feel like your prayers are weak. You can increase the potency of your prayers by writing them clearly and attaching scriptures that support your particular prayer point(s). Eventually, you will find the Holy Spirit taking over and using you to flow in prayer.

If you need a good format to follow, thank God first and foremost because there is always some reason to be thankful. Be humble and ask for forgiveness for doing things your way instead of coming to God. Pray on the scriptures that support your personal desires and requests. You already have the victory when you go to God first in prayer.

For though we walk in the flesh, we are not waging war according to our flesh. For the weapons of our warfare are not of the flesh but have divine power to destroy strongholds.
2 CORINTHIANS 10:3-4 (ESV)

"

YOU ALREADY HAVE THE VICTORY WHEN YOU GO TO GOD FIRST IN PRAYER.

"

Business Meeting Notes

DATE: _____ / ___ / _____

_____
_____
_____
_____
_____
_____
_____
_____
_____
_____
_____
_____
_____
_____
_____
_____
_____
_____
_____
_____
_____
_____
_____

Grace & Forgiveness

God gives you grace even despite occasional disobedience. Christ's sacrifice was an act of grace for all mankind who chose to follow as believers. God wants you to be forgiving as well. He wants you to mend relationships in your life that currently cause you to hold hostility in your heart. He wants us to act as humble servants and exercise grace within any challenging relationships we have.

While we've all been hurt in relationships before, God answers the name Jehovah Rapha, which means the God who heals. He can take away our pains if we ask Him. He corrects your wounds so that painful relationships no longer have control over you or your actions.

Insecurities and imperfections actually affect how we handle relationships. Some people in our lives allow their shortcomings to transform into abusive behavior toward us and others. It is not your responsibility to make up for anyone else's shortcomings. God's Word can set you free from the grips of hostile relationships. He has given us grace before and He will continue to do so today and everyday as long as we place Him in charge of us.

Three times I pleaded with the Lord about this, that it should leave me. But He said to me, "My grace is sufficient for you, for my power is made perfect in weakness." Therefore I will boast all the more gladly of my weaknesses, so that the power of Christ may rest upon me.
2 CORINTHIANS 12:8-9 (ESV)

Do not let any part of your body become an instrument of evil to serve sin. Instead, give yourselves completely to God, for you were dead, but now you have new life. So use your whole body as an instrument to do what is right for the glory of God. Sin is no longer your master, for you no longer live under the requirements of the law. Instead, you live under the freedom of God's grace.
ROMANS 6:13-14 (NLT)

Business Meeting Notes

DATE: ___ / ___ / _____

_____
_____
_____
_____
_____
_____
_____
_____
_____
_____
_____
_____
_____
_____
_____
_____
_____
_____
_____
_____
_____
_____
_____
_____

Command Your Authority

uthority has been given to you over the schemes of the enemy. However, the devil has a crafty approach and will persistently try you in many ways. These attempts aim to overwhelm your senses with grief. Mental anxiety, physical loss, physical pain, and abandonment are a few characteristics of the devil's mark and plan for your life. We covered the name Jehovah Rapha recently. God also goes by the name Jehovah Jireh, which means the Lord will provide. If we're in need of any form of healing, our God is capable. If we feel we've lost anything, our God can replenish and cause favor to runneth over.

The Bible says *"His name Jesus will cast out demons."* By virtue you have the power to cast out demons. The book of Romans says "the God of peace will soon crush Satan under your feet. The grace of our Lord Jesus be with you." You have dominion to keep the devil in his place. Remind yourself that you are victorious because Christ dwells within you. Therefore you will win and will remain separated from harm in every situation. Take time to remind yourself that you are the head and not the tail, and that you are the lender and never the borrower. Let it sink in and stand confidently on what God says since He gives you such authority.

And these signs will accompany those who believe: In my name they will drive out demons; they will speak in new tongues;
MARK 16:17 (NIV)

Finally, be strong in the Lord and in His mighty power. Put on the full armor of God, so that you can take your stand against the devil's schemes. For our struggle is not against flesh and blood, but against the authorities, against the powers of this dark world and against the spiritual forces of evil in the heavenly realms. Therefore put on the full armor of God, so that when the day of evil comes, you may be able to stand your ground, and after you have done everything, to stand. Stand firm then, with the belt of truth buckled around your waist, with the breastplate of righteousness in place, and with your feet fitted with the readiness that comes from the gospel of peace. In addition to all this, take up the shield of faith, with which you can extinguish all the flaming arrows of the evil one. Take the helmet of salvation and the sword of the Spirit, which is the Word of God. And pray in the Spirit on all occasions with all kinds of prayers and requests. With this in mind, be alert and always keep praying for all the Lord's people.
EPHESIANS 6:10-18 (NIV)

Submit yourselves, then, to God. Resist the devil, and he will flee from you.
JAMES 4:7 (NIV)

Business Meeting Notes

DATE: _____ / / _____

_____
_____
_____
_____
_____
_____
_____
_____
_____
_____
_____
_____
_____
_____
_____
_____
_____
_____
_____

The Spirit of God Fuels Your Business

Jesus Christ is the Way, the Truth, and the Light and through prayer God will bless the works of your hands as you take part in your assignment. Every good thing we experience in life are gifts from Him, even the business idea(s) you receive.

Oftentimes we become gripped with excitement when we receive a great idea. The emotion can feel good, but always remember to go back to Him for further consultation. As He gave you the idea, He will also pour out instructions on how to execute and see it through. It takes work to transform an idea into something real and tangible. Therefore, never skip steps related to your assignment area and take heed to God's instruction which will critically serve you throughout the process. He will give you the strength to achieve excellence, so work diligently toward completing the steps He outlines for you. Within God's will, you'll find numerous layers of favor so it is in your best interest to receive those instructions from the source and follow through.

Instead, you ought to say, "If it is the Lord's will, we will live and do this or that."
JAMES 4:15 (NIV)

However, I consider my life worth nothing to me, my only aim is to finish the race and complete the task the Lord Jesus has given me—the task of testifying to the good news of God's grace.
ACTS 20:24 (NIV)

> **EVERY GOOD THING WE EXPERIENCE IN LIFE ARE GIFTS FROM HIM, EVEN THE BUSINESS IDEA(S) YOU RECEIVE.**

Business Meeting Notes

DATE: _____ / / _____

Praise the Most High

Today is a day to worship God! Worship is about positioning your heart to give thanks to God. The book of Romans says that we should offer our bodies as a living sacrifice, holy and pleasing to God, as the proper form of worship. It means recounting everything He's done for you over the past 24 hours alone. It includes reflecting on all He's done for those close to you over the past 24 hours. As you get into it, you lay down everything you love before God who gives us all that we could ever ask for and so much more.

Add worship to your daily life when you wake and acknowledge the fact that He's the one who woke you and kept every surrounding structure in tact while you slept. As you're preparing for the day, be sure to worship and carry it on throughout the day. You have life in your body and strength in your bones! Praise Him for your recent successes and the learning experiences from failed attempts in other areas. There is a lot to be gained from what we view as failures. In fact, those are added opportunities for you to ask Him to guide you through. He won't let you down whenever you call on Him so give Him praise for being loyal to you!

Know therefore that the Lord your God is God; He is the faithful God, keeping His covenant of love to a thousand generations of those who love Him and keep His commandments.
DEUTERONOMY 7:9 (NIV)

Your love, Lord, reaches to the heavens, your faithfulness to the skies.
PSALMS 36:5 (NIV)

66

WORSHIP IS ABOUT POSITIONING YOUR HEART TO GIVE THANKS TO GOD.

99

Business Meeting Notes

DATE: _____ / / _____

The Word Covers Your Life

God's word is a weapon and we have to take it upon ourselves to become familiar with it. Speak the word over your life in the morning, in the afternoon, and in the evening! Devote yourself so much that it opens up refined visions for how God intended your business to be.

The excerpt from 1 Peter above describes the trials that we must all go through before our faith is confirmed. We recently read a scripture from Ephesians 6, that says "…take up the shield of faith, with which you can extinguish all the flaming arrows of the evil one." It's your faith in His word that carries you through. While God makes a way for us out of no way, exercising faith is your responsibility. The fact that you believe in what is not seen, you position yourself to receive your blessings when they have been prepared for you. Ready yourself with the Word and refrain from making excuses for not knowing what the Bible says. You have heaven's angels on your side and knowing the Word aids you in running with them in sync.

For the Word of God is alive and active. Sharper than any double-edged sword, it penetrates even to dividing soul and spirit, joints and marrow; it judges the thoughts and attitudes of the heart. Nothing in all creation is hidden from God's sight. Everything is uncovered and laid bare before the eyes of Him to whom we must give account.
HEBREWS 4:12-13 (NIV)

In all this you greatly rejoice, though now for a little while you may have had to suffer grief in all kinds of trials. These have come so that the proven genuineness of your faith—of greater worth than gold, which perishes even though refined by fire—may result in praise, glory and honor when Jesus Christ is revealed. Though you have not seen Him, you love Him; and even though you do not see Him now, you believe in Him and are filled with an inexpressible and gorious joy, for you are receiving the end result of your faith, the salvation of your souls. Concerning this salvation, the prophets, who spoke of the grace that was to come to you, searched intently and with the greatest care, trying to find out the time and circumstances to which the Spirit of Christ in them was pointing when He predicted the sufferings of the Messiah and the glories that would follow. It was revealed to them that they were not serving themselves but you, when they spoke of the things that have now been told you by those who have preached the gospel to you by the Holy Spirit sent from heaven. Even angels long to look into these things.
1 PETER 1:6-12 (NIV)

Business Meeting Notes

DATE: ___/___/___

_____
_____
_____
_____
_____
_____
_____
_____
_____
_____
_____
_____
_____
_____
_____
_____
_____
_____
_____
_____
_____
_____

Nothing Can Harm What God Has Blessed

God will give you a sense of peace and ease when you're working in your calling. The world we live in is not as kind and gentle as God's loving hand. Along your journey, you will be greeted by naysayers and nonsupporters. You will also find yourself among loved ones who project their own anxieties onto you and what you've been called to do. However, as long as you are present before God, you will receive signs of encouragement that will keep you on pace.

A story of Israel's departure from Egypt in search of new land is told in the book of Numbers, chapters 22 and 23. As they made their way through surrounding territories, there were leaders who wanted to derail their path. These leaders called for curses to be cast onto the Israelites, but it was said that you cannot curse what God has already blessed. The Israelites were indeed governed by God as they moved toward their promised land. In your life, you will be ushered by God, by His angels, and by His messengers toward your promised land. It must be emphasized that what you're working toward is not an easy feat and it will appear nearly impossible to some outsiders looking in. However, certain well-meaning people will be introduced to you; opportunities will present themselves; and you will obtain new levels of favor all because nothing can prevent what has been designed by God.

The Lord will vindicate me; your love, Lord, endures forever—do not abandon the works of your hands.
PSALM 138:8 (NIV)

For this very reason, make every effort to add to your faith goodness; and to goodness, knowledge; and to knowledge, self-control; and to self-control, perseverance; and to perseverance, godliness; and to godliness, mutual affection; and to mutual affection, love. For if you possess these qualities in increasing measure, they will keep you from being ineffective and unproductive in your knowledge of our Lord Jesus Christ. But whoever does not have them is nearsighted and blind, forgetting that they have been cleansed from their past sins.
2 PETER 1:5-9 (NIV)

Business Meeting Notes

DATE: ___ / ___ / ___

Focus on Freedom & Faith

Freedom and self-sufficiency is the goal of every entrepreneur. Having said that, it is our responsibility to separate from ties that hold us in bondage. Oftentimes, we are blinded by a desire for temporary satisfaction from "things". These things may be excessive shopping trips or a bad habit of partying too hard to take your mind off your difficult tasks. These tendencies step in between us and our reliance on faith. Be careful not to engage in a short-term fix that can lead to greater dependency, causing more harm than good.

We must always remember that God is the source of our joy and peace and He shows up on our behalf in the midst of our struggles. Let your faith be your guide as challenges come. Let that stick with you even if you find yourself on a rollercoaster ride, navigating through peaks and valleys. The same path leads you to freedom because of your faith in a God who will fight to get you there.

Along the way, you will venture through unfamiliar environments and will be introduced to new relationships. Everything you go through will be designed to make you stronger and more empathetic. The book of James says that those who endure through trials are the ones who are blessed. They will also receive the crown of life promised by God. Is that something you want? If you answer yes, good! Your fortitude and grit will promote you. Others facing similar struggles will be led to you and you will have the experience and vision to pull them to new heights.

Cast your burden upon the Lord and He will sustain you; He will never allow the righteous to be shaken.
PSALM 55:22 (ESV)

It is for freedom that Christ has set us free. Stand firm, then, and do not let yourselves be burdened again by a yoke of slavery.
GALATIANS 5:1 (NIV)

Business Meeting Notes

DATE: _____ / / _____

_____

_____

_____

_____

_____

_____

_____

_____

_____

_____

_____

_____

_____

_____

_____

_____

_____

_____

_____

_____

_____

_____

Time for Skill and Poise

God provides you with the way and it is your job to follow that path which has been laid out for you. We must take responsibility and use our gifts wisely so as not to squander them. Our great God entrusts us with resources with which we are to be productive and multiply!

The scripture above speaks of a lasting crown that we strive to obtain. In your business, you also seek to obtain a special prize that lasts and the scripture indicates that such a thing is gained through skill and determination. Let's compare this to some common activities:

For anyone who runs, you realize that you must run with purpose and a sense of determination if you expect to finish your route in a decent time. Whenever you run lazily, you wear yourself down even more and might not be able to finish—period. But when you run with poise, with good form and posture, you're able to perform at a level of excellence. That's what determination will do. For anyone who swims (and a lesson for those who don't), you're able to float easily when you move efficiently. Sea creatures have graceful movements but non-swimmers usually get in the water and throw arms, legs, and head frantically all over the place. The aim is not to drown but the lack of skill will cause you to sink and waste energy at the same time. We must develop the skill in our areas of expertise because a crown is not a lasting one if you can't stay afloat.

Though we may think of our progress as running a race, it is most important that we remember to wait on God's timing. He operates differently than us, but it makes time for us to develop our skill while remaining determined. God will add unto you daily with that attitude and will present the lasting crown you seek. Trust in His process and you will see in yourself that you can sustain as a leader in your own right. You will find in your spirit that you can take on bigger challenges than what you had seen before.

Do you not know that in a race all the runners run, but only one gets the prize? Run in such a way as to get the prize. Everyone who competes in the games goes into strict training. They do it to get a crown that will not last, but we do it to get a crown that will last forever. Therefore I do not run like someone running aimlessly;
1 CORINTHIANS 9:24-26 (NIV)

Business Meeting Notes

DATE: _____/____/_____

_____

_____

_____

_____

_____

_____

_____

_____

_____

_____

_____

_____

_____

_____

_____

_____

_____

_____

_____

_____

_____

_____

_____

_____

_____

_____

Abandon Your Fear

t is quite obvious that you are headed somewhere in life as you've gone 30+ days into this devotional. Applaud yourself!

Since the first entry, you've reflected, prayed, committed some things to God and recommitted other things to the Lord. This is a good place for you to sort yourself out. There's a part of you that is becoming and gradually being built in faith. Yet, there still remains an old you that deals with uncomfortable past experiences. We have all faced hardships and some of us have buried our feelings as a coping mechanism. The old saying goes, "everything in the darkness comes out to the light." The same is true for suppressed feelings and reactions that can resurface in different activities and relationships.

You've been able to come this far for a reason. There is still so much to work for and you will encounter challenges in your growth and your new-found identity. Reflect on those buried emotions and evaluate them so that you operate as the new and improved version of you. The scripture above from the book of Mark says that you are not to place new wine into old wineskins which are worn out and no longer applicable to the objective. In the same way, you want to learn from your past to avoid resisting future blessings to come.

No one sews a patch of unshrunk cloth on an old garment. Otherwise, the new piece will pull away from the old, making the tear worse.
MARK 2:21 (NIV)

So, my brothers and sisters, you also died to the law through the body of Christ, that you might belong to another, to Him who was raised from the dead, in order that we might bear fruit for God. For when we were in the realm of the flesh, the sinful passions aroused by the law were at work in us, so that we bore fruit for death. But now, by dying to what once bound us, we have been released from the law so that we serve in the new way of the Spirit, and not in the old way of the written code.
ROMANS 7:4-6 (NIV)

Business Meeting Notes

DATE: _____ / / _____

_____

_____

_____

_____

_____

_____

_____

_____

_____

_____

_____

_____

_____

_____

_____

_____

_____

_____

_____

_____

_____

_____

_____

_____

Power Within Your Flaws

You do great by yourself but you could be a force with the right help. Some of the country's oldest corporations are still here because of growth from reaching out to the public for assistance in their early phases.

We all have our own strengths and weaknesses. Ask God to place people in your life that can directly benefit from your strengths and that can help you in your weak areas. Many times, we become so busy overcompensating for our weaknesses that we lose focus on the things we do best. Remember, we are to be wise with our gifts so as not to squander them, causing us to miss out on our blessings.

None of us is perfect but each one of us has been given free will and wisdom with which to operate. With such a combination, we are able to fill gaps in our lives and create systems for repeated growth and sustainability.

One man of you shall chase a thousand, for the Lord your God is He who fights for you, as He promised you. Therefore take careful heed to yourselves, that you love the Lord your God.
JOSHUA 23:10-11 (NKJV)

And he said to the human race, "The fear of the Lord—that is wisdom, and to shun evil is understanding."
JOB 28:28 (NIV)

Have you not known? Have you not heard? The Lord is the everlasting God, the Creator of the ends of the earth. He does not faint or grow weary; His understanding is unsearchable. He gives power to the faint, and to him who has no might He increases strength. Even youths shall faint and be weary, and young men shall fall exhausted; but they who wait for the Lord shall renew their strength; they shall mount up with wings like eagles; they shall run and not be weary; they shall walk and not faint.
ISAIAH 40:28-31 (ESV)

Business Meeting Notes

DATE: _____ / / _____

_____

_____

_____

_____

_____

_____

_____

_____

_____

_____

_____

_____

_____

_____

_____

_____

_____

_____

_____

_____

_____

Respect God's Time

Organize your schedule so that you don't neglect spending time with God. Take an account of time-consuming activities that draw you away from God. Think about your past month or even your past week and write down how your schedule has gone. When you wake up, are you immediately attending to something? After you address it and you prepare for the day, do you busy yourself with another task? Do this exercise and be sure to record all your general activities and plans from waking up to going to sleep. Does your day become an endless ball of busy work that rolls into the next day? No matter your answer, ask yourself which activities are actually necessary for your well-being. It's easy to get wrapped up in the monotony of our day-to-day and to lose sight of what's really important for us now and for our future. If you can, weed out or cut back on anything that does not add to your purpose in life.

Our greatest example, Jesus Christ, made it clear that our primary goal is to follow the Lord and all other things are secondary. Be mindful of the big picture! Based on the general list you create, do you engage in anything that you put before God? At times, we can find ourselves faced with certain pressures which cause us to be in a state of fight-or-flight. Yet and still, is it fair to Him that you allow anything to take your attention away? He can get you out of any mess you find yourself in as long as you believe in Him. Accept in your heart that God is able to grant you absolute fulfillment for years to come. Give God the attention that He desires from you and it will not be in vain.

But seek first His kingdom and His righteousness, and all these things will be given to you as well.
MATTHEW 6:33 (NIV)

Business Meeting Notes

DATE: _____ / / _____

A Basket Filled with Faithful Prayer Will Bring Much

I t's been said repeatedly in this devotional that we should trust God to provide every resource we need to fulfill our purpose. You might not have role models or abundant funding. In fact, your situation may not be pretty. However, remind yourself that God is our source for all good things. If you earnestly ask Him for direction in prayer, He will not withhold it from you. Allow God to help you see more clearly. Trust Him to guide your steps and you will be led in the right direction at the right time.

In the scripture, Jesus fed thousands of people after giving God thanks. He approached the source and became equipped to feed the masses. Their starting resources, five loaves of bread and two fish, would not have properly fed 20 people, and even if 20 ate, they would not all be satisfied. Later in the next chapter *(MAT 15:32-38)*, He feeds 4,000 people out of a small basket of food. What all this means is that no matter your starting position, or your current position, God will not leave you lacking anything if you approach Him in prayer. With anything you're struggling with, the last scripture applies - seek the kingdom of God first and it shall be well with you.

As evening approached, the disciples came to Him and said, "This is a remote place, and it's already getting late. Send the crowds away, so they can go to the villages and buy themselves some food." Jesus replied, "They do not need to go away. You give them something to eat." "We have here only five loaves of bread and two fish," they answered. "Bring them here to me," He said. And He directed the people to sit down on the grass. Taking the five loaves and the two fish and looking up to heaven, He gave thanks and broke the loaves. Then He gave them to the disciples, and the disciples gave them to the people. They all ate and were satisfied, and the disciples picked up twelve basketfuls of broken pieces that were left over. The number of those who ate was about five thousand men, besides women and children.
MATTHEW 14:15-21 (NIV)

Business Meeting Notes

DATE: _____ / / _____

_____
_____
_____
_____
_____
_____
_____
_____
_____
_____
_____
_____
_____
_____
_____
_____
_____
_____
_____
_____
_____
_____

Pulled from Doom to Glory

Don't underestimate the challenges that you will face along your path. God's process of perfecting you won't be achieved until you go through rough patches. Without the challenges and discomfort, there is no way to understand, appreciate, or identify what perfection is. You must maintain faith throughout tribulations so that it can be validated in your favor. There is never a need for faith if everything goes your way. God does not want you to live a life of complacency, but He wants to prove His glory to His children through you.

No matter what we go through in life, our Father already has the victory. Daniel was thrown into a den with lions but was untouched because God already won. Daniel believed in his heart that he would be saved despite the odds being stacked against him. It takes such resistance to the pressures we face in life for God's acts of power to truly be appreciated. Seek God on your behalf to achieve mighty breakthroughs in the midst of opposition. Attached to your mission is peace for you and an awesome display of glory for Him. With that in mind, execute your mission all the way through its completion and you too will be satisfied by what He prepares for you.

At the first light of dawn, the king got up and hurried to the lions' den. When he came near the den, he called to Daniel in an anguished voice, "Daniel, servant of the living God, has your God, whom you serve continually, been able to rescue you from the lions?" Daniel answered, "May the king live forever! My God sent His angel, and He shut the mouths of the lions..."
DANIEL 6:19-22 (NIV)

66

NO MATTER WHAT WE GO THROUGH IN LIFE, OUR FATHER ALREADY HAS THE VICTORY.

99

Business Meeting Notes

DATE: _____ / / _____

Dreams Tied to Realities

Your dreams will not only play a role in the growth of your business, but they are a key to your existence. Many times, dreams reveal to us a favorable goal(s) that we have not achieved yet. Whenever you day dream, you're looking into a reality that does not completely exist. Internally, it gives you goals to pursue but you are drawn to those desires for a reason. Ask God to give you vision and insight into your dreams to better understand how to become that reality that attracts you so much. You are capable of accomplishing anything with as a child of God having Him on your side.

Daniel's interpretation of a dream set him free from being killed by the king of Babylon. This dream turned his entire destiny around. In the middle of interpreting dreams, Daniel transforms from being a prisoner of Babylon to receiving great gifts from the king. Your dreams are equally as important and shall also do wonders for you. With the help of God almighty, you too can see a steady transformation where you begin living your dream life instead of seeing it only in your head.

Then the secret was revealed to Daniel in a night vision. So Daniel blessed the God of heaven. Daniel answered and said: "Blessed be the name of God forever and ever, For wisdom and might are His. And He changes the times and the seasons; He removes kings and raises up kings; He gives wisdom to the wise And knowledge to those who have understanding. He reveals deep and secret things; He knows what is in the darkness, And light dwells with Him. "I thank You and praise You, O God of my fathers; You have given me wisdom and might, And have now made known to me what we asked of You, For You have made known to us the king's demand."
DANIEL 2:19-23 (NKJV)

The king answered Daniel, and said, "Truly your God is the God of gods, the Lord of kings, and a revealer of secrets, since you could reveal this secret." Then the king promoted Daniel and gave him many great gifts; and he made him ruler over the whole province of Babylon, and chief administrator over all the wise men of Babylon.
DANIEL 2:47-48 (NKJV)

Business Meeting Notes

DATE: ___ / ___ / ___

_____

_____

_____

_____

_____

_____

_____

_____

_____

_____

_____

_____

_____

_____

_____

_____

_____

_____

_____

_____

_____

_____

DAY
37

Never Mind What Others Are Doing

The comparison game is a deceitful measurement of your success. The enemy can use it as a device to fill your spirit with envy. Be careful not to take the bait! Although we are all unique individuals, we are wired to relate with one another. It is better for us to relate empathetically rather than being invested in what belongs to someone else.

One problem with the comparison games is that you never quite know what's attached to that thing that you find desirable. A popular fashion brand on Instagram may encounter inventory issues. A notable restaurant partnership may face constant employee turnover. We are best equipped to walk in our own shoes and not ones made for others.

The scripture above urges you to get busy on your own assignment. It's not easy to execute everything God intends for us, but it's a lot harder when you're attempting to do it exactly how someone else has. God wants you to seek His counsel whenever you need clarity and specifics. Learn your own strengths and weaknesses and operate in what you do best. By operating in your strengths, you'll find yourself in the position to provide services and obtain outcomes better than anyone around you.

Make it your goal to live a quiet life, minding your own business and working with your hands, just as we instructed you before. Then people who are not believers will respect the way you live, and you will not need to depend on others.
1 THESSALONIANS 4:11-12 (NLT)

WE ARE BEST EQUIPPED TO WALK
IN OUR OWN SHOES AND NOT ONES
MADE FOR OTHERS.

Business Meeting Notes

DATE: _____ / / _____

_____
_____
_____
_____
_____
_____
_____
_____
_____
_____
_____
_____
_____
_____
_____
_____
_____
_____
_____
_____
_____
_____
_____
_____

Light Up Your Journey

You have been designed for maturity and growth. This means that at different stages in life, God intends for you to graduate to new levels. In order for us to climb higher, we have to be exposed to new and different things. This is the only way to learn how to maintain our footing on our ascension.

In order to stretch, we have to step out of and other times live outside of our comfort zones. They are called 'comfort zones' for a reason. When you're asked about what you find comfortable, a few things come to mind immediately:

1. Sofa
2. Bed
3. Television
4. Etc.

Your list may be slightly different but there is one main commonality to note. There is little to no activity in a comfort zone. Comfort is associated with words like easy, content, relax, and relief, all of which involve lower levels of activity. In other words, there is a tendency to be stagnant in the comfort zone.

Exposure is key in our growth. Take opportunities to explore your interests, to acquire new tastes, and to gain new insights. God has granted you with freedom to have dominion over the land. Accept His invitation so that the world does not dictate your life to you. When you enter and conquer unfamiliar territory, you can apply meaningful experiences as you continue to climb and grow.

"The lamp of the body is the eye. If therefore your eye is good, your whole body will be full of light."
MATTHEW 6:22 (NKJV)

DAY
39

DATE: _____ / / _____

_____
_____
_____
_____
_____
_____
_____
_____
_____
_____
_____
_____
_____
_____
_____
_____
_____
_____
_____
_____
_____

Look Forward to Your Harvest

Be diligent in applying God's Word to your efforts and He will provide supernatural provisions in your favor. You have a long road ahead in life and in business. We should operate with urgency like the ant who is not lazy. Yet, none of us arrives at the promised land in a single moment. Instead, your greatness comes from strings of mini-moments of excellence.

If you haven't done so already set achievable goals to develop consistency and momentum. If you already have goals, compare your short-term goals with your long-term goals to make sure both are in sync. Do this exercise to map out the growth of your business. Additionally, perform this exercise with your finances. Stewardship over the few will prepare you for what's greater to come. When we define a plan for our finances, we decrease the opportunity for waste. There's an old saying that goes "One who has no plan plans to fail."

Go to the ant, you sluggard; consider its ways and be wise! It has no commander, no overseer or ruler, yet it stores its provisions in summer and gathers its food at harvest.
PROVERBS 6:6-8 (NIV)

Let us not become weary in doing good, for at the proper time we will reap a harvest if we do not give up.
GALATIANS 6:9 (NIV)

...YOUR GREATNESS COMES FROM STRINGS OF MINI-MOMENTS OF EXCELLENCE.

Business Meeting Notes

DATE: _____ / / _____

_____

_____

_____

_____

_____

_____

_____

_____

_____

_____

_____

_____

_____

_____

_____

_____

_____

_____

_____

_____

_____

_____

_____

Always Be the Best You Can Be

In the last entry, we discussed that your greatness in the future is a collection of consistent mini-moments of greatness today. With that in mind, give your best self with every opportunity you have. When you selectively pick the times when you feel like turning on your glow, your muscle memory will not be sharpened as it should.

We never know what our future holds, and we never know when our fortune shifts for the better. In the book of 1 Samuel, David was portrayed to be the least likely to inherit the throne over Israel. His father did not believe, nor did his brothers believe. David proved them wrong on a grand stage when he slayed Goliath with a sling-shot. Yes, David became king but before his fame, David was already accustomed to killing lions and bears that were much stronger than he was. His muscle memory was shaped for his moment of greatness against Goliath. Let today's message encourage you—the stage is not important. It is, however, important for you to showcase your best, leaving nothing to be desired.

Whatever your hand finds to do, do it with all your might, for in the realm of the dead, where you are going, there is neither working nor planning nor knowledge nor wisdom.
ECCLESIASTES 9:10 (NIV)

Whatever you do, work at it with all your heart, as working for the Lord, not for human masters, since you know that you will receive an inheritance from the Lord as a reward. It is the Lord Christ you are serving.
COLOSSIANS 3:23-24 (NIV)

...IMPORTANT FOR YOU TO SHOWCASE YOUR BEST, LEAVING NOTHING TO BE DESIRED.

DAY 41

Business Meeting Notes

DATE: _____/_____/_____

_____

_____

_____

_____

_____

_____

_____

_____

_____

_____

_____

_____

_____

_____

_____

_____

_____

_____

_____

_____

_____

_____

Use It and Don't Lose It

Our past few entries, and other recent ones, have covered how wisdom, diligence, and purpose will impact everything you're working to accomplish. We never know God's timing, but He invites our prayers and helps us learn about our assignment. With that understanding, we can plan, strategize and execute with consistency while waiting on God. Our precious Lord has already endowed us with many gifts and talents. We are to use them intently and He will add on to our talents. Your abilities will increase and your exposure will change as your influence expands.

The bible says that God is the one who gives us the ability to create wealth. He gives us ideas along with the strength and resources to see them through. So when we allow our flame to go out and we find ourselves stagnant with a plan and no follow-through, there's no surprise when we don't see an increase. He recognizes when we are ready to be promoted but we must prove that we are worthy with the small things before expecting something greater. Our training grounds are the small things which in the end will prepare us so that we are not overwhelmed. Without understanding how to utilize our talents and gifts, we have no idea how to utilize all the great opportunities coming our way. Give the Lord all the glory for His will and His dedication to us that we never fail.

"If you are faithful in little things, you will be faithful in large ones. But if you are dishonest in little things, you won't be honest with greater responsibilities. And if you are untrustworthy about worldly wealth, who will trust you with the true riches of heaven? And if you are not faithful with other people's things, why should you be trusted with things of your own? "No one can serve two masters. For you will hate one and love the other; you will be devoted to one and despise the other. You cannot serve God and be enslaved to money."
LUKE 16:10-13 (NLT)

Business Meeting Notes

DATE: _____ / / _____

_____

_____

_____

_____

_____

_____

_____

_____

_____

_____

_____

_____

_____

_____

_____

_____

_____

_____

_____

_____

_____

_____

_____

_____

Wins From Losses

By this point in your life, you have come to learn that we can't always have everything how we would like it to be. We find it challenging at the onset of our loss of friendships, money, cars, furniture, etc. The initial shock of having to part with our loss is followed by how to replace it. Once the realization settles in, you will find one of two things—your loss had value or your loss did not have the value you believed it had.

Today, we're focusing on the loss of things. Jehovah Jireh is our provider and gives us all that we need. He gives us everything to fulfill our heart desires. Our own personal interests can distract us at times. In the previous entry, the scripture selection closed by saying that we cannot serve God and serve money. This goes for the things money can buy like cars, clothes, and jewelry. The reality of losing "things" is that they weigh us down if we're not paying attention. The car that you were drawn toward required higher insurance premiums that you had to cover. The outfit you wore attracted more physical attention as opposed to keeping you focused on your assignment. An old friend took more of your time than necessary because they needed to talk to you about their problems. This general list may apply to you or you have your own set.

Some of the losses we experience actually turn out to be gains. We live in a world full of distractions and we don't need to be responsible for bringing any more of them into our own camp. The simple things we own and use are the cornerstones of our innovation. They help us to create the life we want to live. They open the door for our gifts to pave the way for us. They keep the door open for God to provide for us, to replenish our stock, and to satisfy our hearts.

For no one can lay any foundation other than the one already laid, which is Jesus Christ. If anyone builds on this foundation using gold, silver, costly stones, wood, hay or straw, their work will be shown for what it is, because the Day will bring it to light. It will be revealed with fire, and the fire will test the quality of each person's work. If what has been built survives, the builder will receive a reward. If it is burned up, the builder will suffer loss but yet will be saved—even though only as one escaping through the flames.
1 CORINTHIANS 3:11-15 (NIV)

Business Meeting Notes

DATE: _____ / / _____

_____

_____

_____

_____

_____

_____

_____

_____

_____

_____

_____

_____

_____

_____

_____

_____

_____

_____

_____

_____

_____

_____

Heart Check Part 2

We are near the halfway mark of our 90 days and now is a good time to perform an evaluation. Have you noticed any changes that feel permanent? In the last entry, we discussed how some losses are actual gains. Those losses are sometimes out of our control but the theory can also apply to anything we decide to release. We carry unnecessary burdens all the time and we can decide to release them when we identify them as such. Have you knowingly let go of anything that held you back? The real question of course is around your relationship with God. Have you relinquished control or are you still wrestling with Him over your responsibilities?

The purpose of this devotional is to help you let go where you want to dominate your own business. Look at the results you've recorded over the past 40+ days. Do you think that more is possible? The actual answer is yes!! Yes because God is omnipotent and can do all things extensively above our expectations. For you to achieve greater results, you will need to look at the areas that you still consider yourself to be a decision maker. If the Lord has specific instructions for you, you better believe that you need to apply them.

It's critical to realize that you can't achieve mighty results when you skip steps. If you need to set aside additional time with God, please do so. You want to be able to hear from Him clearly without being restricted by your plans and competing interests. He wants you to prosper and this may require you to adjust your current processes.

The entrance of Your words gives light; It gives understanding to the simple. I opened my mouth and panted, For I longed for Your commandments. Look upon me and be merciful to me, as Your custom is toward those who love Your name. Direct my steps by Your word, And let no iniquity have dominion over me. Redeem me from the oppression of man, That I may keep Your precepts. Make Your face shine upon Your servant, And teach me Your statutes.
PSALMS 119:130-135 (NKJV)

Business Meeting Notes

DAY
44

DATE: _____/_____/_____

_____
_____
_____
_____
_____
_____
_____
_____
_____
_____
_____
_____
_____
_____
_____
_____
_____
_____
_____
_____
_____
_____
_____
_____

Your Flesh Is Not A Leader

As a reminder, the purpose of this devotional is to bring you to understand why God should be in charge of your business. Ask yourself two things: Are you battling with God and the plans He has for you? Do you pull yourself away from the direction He leads you?

The line of questioning is for you to reflect. God pushes us to land by running streams. God is for us, and we have to work to keep our flesh subdued. Our fleshly desires accept temporary satisfaction over God's everlasting gifts. The flesh can persuade us to give up when the struggle seems to be too much. God's grace contradicts quitting, as He is able to do what people may find impossible. Without Him we tend to gravitate toward meaningless distractions.

As you seek to do what God approves, make a conscious effort to pull farther from your flesh and to pull closer to the Lord Almighty! It will surely take time but a legacy is not created instantly. Follow God's leadership without straying away.

Therefore, there is now no condemnation for those who are in Christ Jesus, because through Christ Jesus the law of the Spirit who gives life has set you free from the law of sin and death. For what the law was powerless to do because it was weakened by the flesh, God did by sending His own Son in the likeness of sinful flesh to be a sin offering. And so He condemned sin in the flesh, in order that the righteous requirement of the law might be fully met in us, who do not live according to the flesh but according to the Spirit. Those who live according to the flesh have their minds set on what the flesh desires; but those who live in accordance with the Spirit have their minds set on what the Spirit desires. The mind governed by the flesh is death, but the mind governed by the Spirit is life and peace. The mind governed by the flesh is hostile to God; it does not submit to God's law, nor can it do so. Those who are in the realm of the flesh cannot please God. You, however, are not in the realm of the flesh but are in the realm of the Spirit, if indeed the Spirit of God lives in you. And if anyone does not have the Spirit of Christ, they do not belong to Christ. But if Christ is in you, then even though your body is subject to death because of sin, the Spirit gives life because of righteousness. And if the Spirit of Him who raised Jesus from the dead is living in you, He who raised Christ from the dead will also give life to your mortal bodies because of His Spirit who lives in you. Therefore, brothers and sisters, we have an obligation—but it is not to the flesh, to live according to it. For if you live according to the flesh, you will die; but if by the Spirit you put to death the misdeeds of the body, you will live.
ROMANS 8:1-13 (NIV)

Business Meeting Notes

DATE: _____ / / _____

_____
_____
_____
_____
_____
_____
_____
_____
_____
_____
_____
_____
_____
_____
_____
_____
_____
_____
_____
_____
_____

Time With God

Build your schedule around God and allow ample time to enter into His presence without distractions. Prepare your days in such a way that you routinely spend time with God. This could be early in the morning before your day begins, late in the evening as a debrief, or even in the mid-day as a break from your day-to-day.

The aim of giving God more of your time is for you to let Him order your steps in the near future as well as in the long term. If your schedule has a poor design, you will be left playing catch-up. The more you give up control, and the more you hand over to God, the better it will be for you.

When you place God in the driver's seat of your time, He will open your eyes so that your focus is on the important things. He will give you peace along with patience despite the daily rat race. Much of our stress really comes when our attention is diverted away from our priorities. God's governance will reduce your anxiety and will increase assurance that you are on the right path. The time you spend with God can do nothing but benefit you cause.

I am with you and will watch over you wherever you go, and I will bring you back to this land. I will not leave you until I have done what I have promised you." When Jacob awoke from his sleep, he thought, "Surely the Lord is in this place, and I was not aware of it." He was afraid and said, "How awesome is this place! This is none other than the house of God; this is the gate of heaven.
GENESIS 28:15-17 (NIV)

The Lord replied, "My Presence will go with you, and I will give you rest."
EXODUS 33:14 (NIV)

Business Meeting Notes

DATE: ___/___/___

_____
_____
_____
_____
_____
_____
_____
_____
_____
_____
_____
_____
_____
_____
_____
_____
_____
_____
_____
_____

The Ten Percent Perspective Shift

The devil is always busy and will make every attempt to disrupt you by attacking your world. He uses the systems of the world—advertising, finance, government, education, etc.—in discreet ways in hopes of separating us from our peace and our joy. The enemy doesn't hesitate to attack the things we find valuable. If successful, the devil can frustrate us by destroying our valuable belongings. We own things that can expire, break, burn, or otherwise fail, and the enemy can't wait to test us in such a way.

Tithing is a way to protect your business and your personal finances. When you give your 10% back to the kingdom, you are storing up in a safe place where your real blessings come from. Ten percent is no small amount so it takes devotion to part ways with it. By faithfully giving your earnings to the Lord, you are expressing your devotion and commitment to God's word. In addition, your tithes and offerings take away from the devil's operations. He licks his chops to attach those physical things you've accumulated. When you divert 10% for tithing, you shut away your vulnerability to the devil's plan while opening doors accessing God's kingdom as long as you're able.

Don't be deceived, my dear brothers and sisters. Every good and perfect gift is from above, coming down from the Father of the heavenly lights, who does not change like shifting shadows. He chose to give us birth through the word of truth, that we might be a kind of firstfruits of all he created.
JAMES 1:16-18 (NIV)

66

BY FAITHFULLY GIVING YOUR EARNINGS TO THE LORD, YOU ARE EXPRESSING YOUR DEVOTION AND COMMITMENT TO GOD'S WORD.

99

Business Meeting Notes

DATE: ___/___/___

_____
_____
_____
_____
_____
_____
_____
_____
_____
_____
_____
_____
_____
_____
_____
_____
_____
_____
_____
_____
_____
_____

Strong Enough to Power You

Strategizing is a key aspect of business. When done properly, we are able to make rational and calculated decisions instead of emotional ones. Our strategy puts us in a better position to obtain an outcome close to our expectations. But sometimes our plans don't pan out as we intended and we face disappointments. It may feel that all is lost but we have to endure as the race does not go to the swiftest.

Disappointments cause temporary road closures but we can find the correct detour. What is important is our ability to endure when times get tough. We've recently discussed the importance of trusting God who is capable of all things. He is strong in our weakness and when you face difficult seasons, remember these two things:

1. God sees you as special and valuable
2. God will not place you in situations that you cannot handle

Because God is on your side, you can lean on Him for that endurance and perseverance. Remember those two points above as you seek favor from Him even in your time of need. You are a special part of God's kingdom and your success adds to His Glory.

In those days, Hezekiah became ill and was at the point of death. The prophet Isaiah son of Amoz went to him and said, "This is what the Lord says. Put your house in order, because you are going to die; you will not recover." Hezekiah turned his face to the wall and prayed to the Lord, "Remember, Lord, how I have walked before you faithfully and with wholehearted devotion and have done what is good in your eyes." And Hezekiah wept bitterly. Before Isaiah had left the middle court, the word of the Lord came to him: "Go back and tell Hezekiah, the ruler of my people, This is what the Lord, the God of your father David, says: I have heard your prayer and seen your tears; I will heal you. On the third day from now you will go up to the temple of the Lord. I will add fifteen years to your life. And I will deliver you and this city from the hand of the king of Assyria.
2 KINGS 20:1-6 (NIV)

Business Meeting Notes

DATE: ___ / / ___

_____
_____
_____
_____
_____
_____
_____
_____
_____
_____
_____
_____
_____
_____
_____
_____
_____
_____
_____
_____
_____
_____
_____
_____

Valued Relationships

Your relationship with God is not comparable to any other one you could have. He is a giving God and we can't begin to repay Him. This is the only relationship where you will receive charity in times where you are undeserving. May He continue to demonstrate His glory in your life! While He is perfect, our other relationships are not and must be managed and here's how.

Identify your current relationships whether long-term or recent ones. Pray over the relationships that come to mind. God will actually give you clarity on those that you need to work to actively grow as well as those that hinder your personal progress as a leader. Analyzing your relationships is not something you'll want to gloss over. They can provide a lot to gain, whether through support or through lessons learned.

Do you have mentors who share relatable wisdom and experiences? Do you have helpful people who provide support? These are certainly two types of relationships that can assist you to new levels. Do you have friendships that drain your energy meaninglessly? This could lead to less productivity and advancement toward your goals and you have to pray on ways to mitigate this particular relationship(s).

Walk with the wise and become wise, for a companion of fools suffers harm.
PROVERBS 13:20 (NIV)

As iron sharpens iron, so one person sharpens another.
PROVERBS 27:17 (NIV)

And let us consider how we may spur one another on toward love and good deeds, not giving up meeting together, as some are in the habit of doing, but encouraging one another—and all the more as you see the Day approaching.
HEBREWS 10:24-25 (NIV)

Business Meeting Notes

DATE: _____ / / _____

Your Build-Up to Prominence

God has brought you this far because He has enormous plans for you. You are probably able to recall any answered prayers because He has introduced you to His power and glory. The key word here is 'introduced.' Yes, He has enormous plans for you! Are you willing to prepare for everything you are asking God to do for you?

If you believe the answer is yes then you have to commit to all the spiritual changes necessary to handle the full calling. Without the proper foundation, you would be at a disadvantage were you to receive the fullness of His blessings. You would find it hard to utilize and sustain the increase. The bible suggests that we need the proper wineskins to contain wine. For new wine, we need new wineskins and not old and used wineskins that would burst under pressure. New wine in a new wineskin ensures that both remain intact. We've all heard countless stories of lottery winners who blow through funds so quickly they have nothing to show for it.

God is working on your behalf. In order for you to handle your increase, you have to grow as a person. Ask God to mold you into the person that He intends for you to be. Actively work on becoming that person and commit to the change process. The growth that you experience will positively affect all areas of your life. Only then will you appreciate and properly manage the overflow of favor He will provide.

Do your planning and prepare your fields before building your house.
PROVERBS 24:27 (NLT)

IN ORDER FOR YOU TO HANDLE YOUR INCREASE,
YOU HAVE TO GROW AS A PERSON.

Business Meeting Notes

DATE: _____ / / _____

Stand by Your Creator

The scripture below clearly defines what we've discussed recently about spending quality time with the Lord. This friendship is one like no other as it strengthens you while enriching you. The scripture draws the line regarding our natural reaction of doing things our way. It says a branch that loses connection from the vine is fruitless. We must develop the habit of seeking Him continuously.

As part of our commitment to God, we hand Him the keys to our life. He drives our day from morning to night. When we seek Him, we tell Him our desires and we ask Him to direct us. If we make it our business to go where He tells us, we find ourselves in less situations where we are forced to make immediate decisions. You don't have to wait until you need a miracle to reach out to God but He can place you on the road to your happiness now.

He does not want to treat you as a slave but wants you to build the friendship. It begins with quality time!

"I am the true grapevine, and my Father is the gardener. He cuts off every branch of mine that doesn't produce fruit, and he prunes the branches that do bear fruit so they will produce even more. You have already been pruned and purified by the message I have given you. Remain in me, and I will remain in you. For a branch cannot produce fruit if it is severed from the vine, and you cannot be fruitful unless you remain in me. "Yes, I am the vine; you are the branches. Those who remain in me, and I in them, will produce much fruit. For apart from me you can do nothing.
Anyone who does not remain in me is thrown away like a useless branch and withers. Such branches are gathered into a pile to be burned. But if you remain in me and my words remain in you, you may ask for anything you want, and it will be granted! When you produce much fruit, you are my true disciples. This brings great glory to my Father. "I have loved you even as the Father has loved me. Remain in my love. When you obey my commandments, you remain in my love, just as I obey my Father's commandments and remain in his love. I have told you these things so that you will be filled with my joy. Yes, your joy will overflow! This is my commandment: Love each other in the same way I have loved you. There is no greater love than to lay down one's life for one's friends. You are my friends if you do what I command.
I no longer call you slaves, because a master doesn't confide in his slaves. Now you are my friends, since I have told you everything the Father told me. You didn't choose me. I chose you. I appointed you to go and produce lasting fruit, so that the Father will give you whatever you ask for, using my name. This is my command: Love each other.
JOHN 15:1-17 (NLT)

Business Meeting Notes

DATE: ___ / ___ / ___

_____

_____

_____

_____

_____

_____

_____

_____

_____

_____

_____

_____

_____

_____

_____

_____

_____

_____

_____

_____

_____

DAY 51

Serve to Surpass

In business, you can't underestimate the value of serving others. The scripture notes that Jesus did not come to be served. He was proactive to serve because through such acts, so much more was gained. Through service, He was able to preach the gospel to many and perform miracles for those in need.

Right now you have a few contacts who have performed in your industry for years. Reach out to them and find out how you could serve them. It's a small gesture on your part that could greatly impact your future. By doing so, the exposure would leave you with useful takeaways while affording you visibility within the industry. In addition to being able to build healthy working relationships with your contacts and increasing your network, at the very least, you will learn how to better speak the language of your business. Learning experiences should not be taken lightly as they add to your expertise which pays many dividends in the end.

For even the Son of Man came not to be served but to serve others and to give His life as a ransom for many.
MARK 10:45 (NLT)

> **HE [JESUS] WAS PROACTIVE TO SERVE BECAUSE THROUGH SUCH ACTS, SO MUCH MORE WAS GAINED.**

Business Meeting Notes

DATE: ___/___/___

_____
_____
_____
_____
_____
_____
_____
_____
_____
_____
_____
_____
_____
_____
_____
_____
_____
_____
_____
_____
_____

Mind Your Development

Continuous improvement (CI) is a common business term defined as an ongoing effort to improve products, services, or processes through "incremental" improvement over time or "breakthrough" improvement all at once. The associated method for CI is plan > do > check > adjust. Businesses develop periodic goals, perform the related tasks, evaluate the results and determine which adjustments to implement moving forward to increase effectiveness for the subsequent period goals.

The scriptures above state that good can't come from rotten, and rotten can't come from good. With that in mind, you can't separate the growth of your business from personal growth as your business is an extension of you. Although none of us is perfect, we all have the daily opportunity to build on our relationship with our Creator who can cleanse us from within. We have to put in work for the Holy Spirit to truly shine through us.

Here is how it all connects: Your personal character dictates the decisions you make. The decisions lead to actions which form your reputation. If you have a reputation as a negative person, you might not be able to appeal to your customer base the way you would like. If you have a reputation for slandering competitors, you may not appear trustworthy. Ultimately, you have to be at peace with yourself if you want to operate at a high level. Your overall ability to perform and function in any area of your life depends on your personal development. While business trainings and seminars can be beneficial, make an equal effort to develop from your spirit within.

You can identify them by their fruit, that is, by the way they act. Can you pick grapes from thornbushes, or figs from thistles? A good tree produces good fruit, and a bad tree produces bad fruit. A good tree can't produce bad fruit, and a bad tree can't produce good fruit.
MATTHEW 7:16-18 (NLT)

"Either make the tree good and its fruit good, or make the tree bad and its fruit bad, for the tree is known by its fruit. You brood of vipers! How can you speak good, when you are evil? For out of the abundance of the heart the mouth speaks. The good person out of his good treasure brings forth good, and the evil person out of his evil treasure brings forth evil.
MATTHEW 12:33-35 (AMP)

Business Meeting Notes

DATE: ___/___/___

Make God's Wisdom A Thing

The bible says that wisdom is the fear of the Lord. He gives us assignments, messages, and many signs. Should we choose to ignore any of them, we risk being tossed into troubled waters. We ask Him to guide our steps but It is up to us to decide that we will listen. We can't afford blown assignments if we are pursuing Him and all His splendor.

The peace that you are promised is contingent upon your obedience. Every time you disobey the calling on your life, you inch closer to the point of no return. God reaches out to us every moment of our lives but when we decide to pull away, we show our ignorance which could be rooted in underlying pain and insecurity. But God is a healer! He will work on our behalf to make us wholesome. Without Him, we don't have much to expect but with Him we have much to gain. This entry is a message for you not to take your calling lightly. God wants you to perform above your own expectations but the only way to know how to reach such heights is for you to pull closer to Him with every opportunity you have.

Pray at times you wouldn't normally pray. Research biblical stories and principles to learn things that you didn't already know. This will load your tongue to speak the blessings of the Word over your day(s).

Come and listen to my counsel. I'll share my heart with you and make you wise. "I called you so often, but you wouldn't come. I reached out to you, but you paid no attention. You ignored my advice and rejected the correction I offered. So I will laugh when you are in trouble! I will mock you when disaster overtakes you— when calamity overtakes you like a storm, when disaster engulfs you like a cyclone, and anguish and distress overwhelm you. "When they cry for help, I will not answer. Though they anxiously search for me, they will not find me. For they hated knowledge and chose not to fear the Lord. They rejected my advice and paid no attention when I corrected them. Therefore, they must eat the bitter fruit of living their own way, choking on their own schemes. For simpletons turn away from me—to death. Fools are destroyed by their own complacency. But all who listen to me will live in peace, untroubled by fear of harm."
PROVERBS 1:23-33 (NLT)

Business Meeting Notes

DATE: _____ / / _____

_____

_____

_____

_____

_____

_____

_____

_____

_____

_____

_____

_____

_____

_____

_____

_____

_____

_____

_____

_____

_____

_____

_____

You Shall Be Comforted

In growing your relationship with God it is likely that you feel vulnerable at times. Steer away from anyone who causes you to feel uncomfortable as your relationship develops. God is a refuge for us; He is a loving God and He is a merciful God. Be careful with other "spiritual" people if they make you feel confused about seeking after God.

The enemy will work through people to deter you from seeking God's shelter and provisions. These are wolves in sheep's clothing who may even show up disguised as a "Christian". Learn to use discernment and to navigate through such traps. Lean on prayer so that you can see through traps. God will speak to you through prayer, revealing truths that confirm your true calling and giving you real comfort.

Dear friends, do not believe everyone who claims to speak by the Spirit. You must test them to see if the spirit they have comes from God. For there are many false prophets in the world. This is how we know if they have the Spirit of God: If a person claiming to be a prophet acknowledges that Jesus Christ came in a real body, that person has the Spirit of God. But if someone claims to be a prophet and does not acknowledge the truth about Jesus, that person is not from God. Such a person has the spirit of the Antichrist, which you heard is coming into the world and indeed is already here. But you belong to God, my dear children. You have already won a victory over those people, because the Spirit who lives in you is greater than the spirit who lives in the world. Those people belong to this world, so they speak from the world's viewpoint, and the world listens to them. But we belong to God, and those who know God listen to us. If they do not belong to God, they do not listen to us. That is how we know if someone has the Spirit of truth or the spirit of deception.
1 JOHN 4:1-6 (NLT)

Business Meeting Notes

DATE: _____/___/_____

_____
_____
_____
_____
_____
_____
_____
_____
_____
_____
_____
_____
_____
_____
_____
_____
_____
_____
_____
_____
_____
_____

Alone Yet Unafraid

There is a two-way relationship that connects us with our blessings. Jesus Christ gave His life for our redemption. From His sacrifice, we gained access to the Father in heaven who is the keeper of every good thing we desire in life. That is one side of the relationship. The second part, which is ours, is our faith that Jesus opened up the way for our victory.

The key here is that it's not someone else's faith that will solidify your blessings. Instead, this is based on your own personal revelation. Your faith will have to be put to the test before it is confirmed. Don't become disheartened if you ever feel you are the only one experiencing a hardship at any point in time. Accept it as part of the process to confirm your faith. There are lessons you will have to learn on your own and it is expected that you persevere and endure through the test to receive your blessing(s). God has plans for each person on this earth and each person will learn lessons at different times and in different ways.

But when you pray, go away by yourself, shut the door behind you, and pray to your Father in private. Then your Father, who sees everything, will reward you.
MATTHEW 6:6 (NLT)

Consider it pure joy, my brothers and sisters, whenever you face trials of many kinds, because you know that the testing of your faith produces perseverance. Let perseverance finish its work so that you may be mature and complete, not lacking anything.
JAMES 1:2-4 (NIV)

66

DON'T BECOME DISHEARTENED IF YOU EVER FEEL YOU ARE THE ONLY ONE EXPERIENCING A HARDSHIP AT ANY POINT IN TIME.

99

Business Meeting Notes

DATE: ___/___/___

_____
_____
_____
_____
_____
_____
_____
_____
_____
_____
_____
_____
_____
_____
_____
_____
_____
_____
_____
_____

Serve as God's Prize

God wants to show you off so He can win souls! You are a gateway for Him to reach those who do not have a deep and trusting personal connection with Him. For this reason, you can trust that He will go to bat for you at any cost. God wants to showcase you as His prized possession and will therefore deliver on your behalf leaving you with numerous testimonies.

Have you experienced any recent breakthroughs? Are there any that come to mind over the past year or month? Whether small or large, God is guiding you, molding you, and keeping you from harm's way for you and others to be a witness to His glory. Do not be afraid to allow Him to use you. He will fight any opposition on your behalf, and through your faith and perseverance, His will can be fulfilled in your life.

The Lord your God is with you, the Mighty Warrior who saves. He will take great delight in you; in His love he will no longer rebuke you, but will rejoice over you with singing."
ZEPHANIAH 3:17 (NIV)

He chose to give us birth through the word of truth, that we might be a kind of firstfruits of all He created.
JAMES 1:18 (NIV)

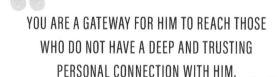

YOU ARE A GATEWAY FOR HIM TO REACH THOSE WHO DO NOT HAVE A DEEP AND TRUSTING PERSONAL CONNECTION WITH HIM.

Business Meeting Notes

DATE: ___ / ___ / ___

Unfathomable Favor

We've touched on the subject of confidence indirectly, but how confident are you in your abilities? How would you rank your level of confidence in God being our provider, healer, and comforter whenever we call on Him? This may be a time to think about the answer to these questions on a deeper level. Are you experiencing anything that causes you to doubt God's great plans for your future?

The scripture above is an excerpt for the wonderful way God wants to treat you. You have to stand firm in your belief that all things will work together for your good. God created heaven, earth, and everything in between. There are no financial issues that can stop His grace! There are no education qualifications to keep Him from promoting you and your cause. There is nothing any government can put in place that stops the blessings of His kingdom. This scripture is a call for you to embrace God's power and reject any force that makes you believe that you are incapable of receiving His favor. With God, all things are possible. His gifts are beyond what you can comprehend.

I pray that out of His glorious riches He may strengthen you with power through His Spirit in your inner being, so that Christ may dwell in your hearts through faith. And I pray that you, being rooted and established in love, may have power, together with all the Lord's holy people, to grasp how wide and long and high and deep is the love of Christ, and to know this love that surpasses knowledge—that you may be filled to the measure of all the fullness of God. Now to Him who is able to do immeasurably more than all we ask or imagine, according to His power that is at work within us, to Him be glory in the church and in Christ Jesus throughout all generations, for ever and ever! Amen.
EPHESIANS 3:16-21 (NIV)

Business Meeting Notes

DATE: _____ / / _____

_____
_____
_____
_____
_____
_____
_____
_____
_____
_____
_____
_____
_____
_____
_____
_____
_____
_____
_____
_____
_____
_____
_____

Let Your Gifts Shine

God designed you in His likeness and that is something that you should never forget. He endowed you with certain gifts that you are to use. Are there any insecurities that interfere with you working in your strength? Think about it and find what they could be. It is important in this season that you root out anything that is not indicative of God's nature from which you were created. Right now is the time to pour your all into your gifts without forming an excuse to hold back.

Any insecurity that you have causes you to act with caution and to think twice when it is time to perform. Remove doubts, and stop dwelling on your flaws because we all have them. Remove whatever resistance and utilize every part of you within your gift. The way you were created is so much more important as the gifts you have been blessed with will make a way for you. You will be sought after for the value you bring.

Each of you should use whatever gift you have received to serve others, as faithful stewards of God's grace in its various forms. If anyone speaks, they should do so as one who speaks the very words of God. If anyone serves, they should do so with the strength God provides, so that in all things God may be praised through Jesus Christ. To Him be the glory and the power for ever and ever. Amen.
1 PETER 4:10-11 (NIV)

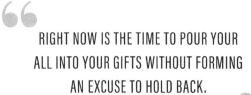

RIGHT NOW IS THE TIME TO POUR YOUR
ALL INTO YOUR GIFTS WITHOUT FORMING
AN EXCUSE TO HOLD BACK.

Business Meeting Notes

DATE: ___/___/___

He Works in Strange Ways

We discussed confidence and how important it is to be confident and wait on the Lord. Make no mistake—you will be tested on many levels. You won't always have the people around you to help you with your challenges. You will have to take many of those challenges on the chin and keep moving.

You will undoubtedly experience spiritual attacks on your mindset to derail you. Times may come where you may consider quitting the race or throwing in the towel. You can endure through those attacks. Maintain an active prayer life and stray away from a defeated position. Yes, show up humbly before God and believe that your prayers are being heard. This type of confidence in your prayers demonstrates your faith. You know that your faith is the very trait that God will use to build your desires out before your eyes. If you are going through a test, there will be a day where you explain to someone how "God works in funny ways".

"Truly I tell you, if anyone says to this mountain, 'Go throw yourself into the sea,' and does not doubt in their heart but believes that what they say will happen, it will be done for them. Therefore I tell you, whatever you ask for in prayer, believe that you have received it, and it will be yours.
MARK 11:23 (NIV)

66

YOU KNOW THAT YOUR FAITH IS THE VERY TRAIT THAT GOD WILL USE TO BUILD YOUR DESIRES OUT BEFORE YOUR EYES.

99

Business Meeting Notes

DATE: ___/___/___

_____

_____

_____

_____

_____

_____

_____

_____

_____

_____

_____

_____

_____

_____

_____

_____

_____

_____

_____

_____

_____

_____

_____

Be Mindful of the Fruits of Your Labor

Are you ignoring signs from God that you are not living the way He wants you to live? Are you finding that you expend your energy in areas that are not working out? Call on God so that He can clarify your purpose to you. Anytime you operate outside of your purpose, it will feel like an uphill battle with no fruits from your work. You will feel as though all your efforts are pointless and could even face danger as a result of chasing the wind. Before he was Paul, Saul was disobedient along with many others in his circle. Some paid with their lives, but Paul became one of the most influential spokesmen for the gospel.

Call on God to redirect your energy so that you find yourself making a meaningful impact. God does not want you to slave and toil over tasks that bring zero joy to you. If you find yourself serving others and you have no accompanying joy, you're hurting yourself and others in the process. Stop ignoring the signs and call on Him to put you on the correct path. In your road to growth, you will experience many times when you must pivot. Trust that God will give you grace when you find that you need to make adjustments.

Meanwhile, Saul was still breathing out murderous threats against the Lord's disciples. He went to the high priest and asked him for letters to the synagogues in Damascus, so that if he found any there who belonged to the Way, whether men or women, he might take them as prisoners to Jerusalem. As he neared Damascus on his journey, suddenly a light from heaven flashed around him. He fell to the ground and heard a voice say to him, "Saul, Saul, why do you persecute me?" "Who are you, Lord?" Saul asked. "I am Jesus, whom you are persecuting," He replied. "Now get up and go into the city, and you will be told what you must do." The men traveling with Saul stood there speechless; they heard the sound but did not see anyone. Saul got up from the ground, but when he opened his eyes he could see nothing. So they led him into Damascus. For three days he was blind, and did not eat or drink anything.
ACTS 9:1-9 (NIV)

Business Meeting Notes

DATE: _____ / / _____

Grace-Filled Experience

God has set aside a life of gain an abundance on our behalf. We must still grow into that lifestyle personally and through the Word. Every one of us is a culmination of all our experiences. By seeking and building of the Word, you position yourself to key in on those experiences God intends for you to go through and to learn from. This is the actual knowledge that will prepare us for the gain and abundance mentioned above. In essence we want to live and experience His word.

Separate from God, the "world" has experiences designed for you too. Worldly attractions cause us to stumble where you can easily find opportunities to lose our money, our discipline, and our focus. It offers many traps to keep us mentally occupied where we find ourselves going in circles to get back to square one.

When we surrender ourselves, becoming planted in God's Word, we can then live God's words. This alignment lets us experience His constant and loving grace.

You adulterous people, don't you know that friendship with the world means enmity against God? Therefore, anyone who chooses to be a friend of the world becomes an enemy of God.
JAMES 4:4 (NIV)

Do not conform to the pattern of this world, but be transformed by the renewing of your mind. Then you will be able to test and approve what God's will is—His good, pleasing and perfect will.
ROMANS 12:2 (NIV)

Take delight in the Lord, and He will give you the desires of your heart.
PSALM 37:4 (NIV)

Business Meeting Notes

DATE: _____/_____/_____

_____

_____

_____

_____

_____

_____

_____

_____

_____

_____

_____

_____

_____

_____

_____

_____

_____

_____

_____

_____

_____

_____

_____

_____

Wait On Him

We continue to describe lessons to be learned from our experiences as believers. It cannot be overstated that we will face adversity even after committing to follow God. Don't be mislead to believe that every day will be perfect. While we are made by our experiences, we are defined by how we react when we do encounter adversity.

If we look into the scripture above, let's imagine how Abraham must have felt when he was told to sacrifice his beloved son. There is no way he was excited to go through with it but he demonstrated his faith in the purpose of the task. So even for us, we go through times where we are out of it and down in the dumps. The lesson comes from how we handle our distress. God wants us to learn to be patient when things don't look how you want them to look. Those make-or-break experiences become our teachable moments that lead to turning-points in life.

> But the angel of the Lord called out to him from heaven, "Abraham! Abraham!" "Here I am," he replied. "Do not lay a hand on the boy," he said. "Do not do anything to him. Now I know that you fear God, because you have not withheld from me your son, your only son." Abraham looked up and there in a thicket he saw a ram caught by its horns. He went over and took the ram and sacrificed it as a burnt offering instead of his son. So Abraham called that place The Lord Will Provide. And to this day it is said, "On the mountain on the Lord it will be provided." The angel of the Lord called to Abraham from heaven a second time and said, "I swear by myself, declares the Lord, that because you have done this and have not withheld your son, your only son, I will surely bless you and make your descendants as numerous as the stars in the sky and as the sand on the seashore. Your descendants will take possession of the cities of their enemies, and through your offspring all nations on earth will be blessed, because you have obeyed me."
> GENESIS 22:11-18 (NIV)

Business Meeting Notes

DATE: _____ / / _____

Never For the Love of Money

As a believer, you can be assured that Jehovah Jireh is indeed your provider and that He will give you everything you need. God becomes our riches when we commit ourselves to Him. He ensures our bills are paid off. He installs safety and security in our life. He promotes us, giving us an increase at the right time, and prepares prosperity for our future.

"Money" as we know it comes today and is gone tomorrow. We can't let the love for money become our motivation for life decisions. Such a love should not be in our heart nor should it be a stimulating force in life. Don't allow money to govern your relationships which should be based on the content of one's character. God's plans for you include money for various reasons. He also has plans that will require other resource types. He will not withhold anything from you but you also must love Him above all else.

You must see Him as your provider and wait as you receive everything you need for His blessings to manifest.

No one can serve two masters. Either you will hate the one and love the other, or you will be devoted to the one and despise the other. You cannot serve both God and money.
MATTHEW 6:24 (NIV)

But store up for yourselves treasures in heaven where moths and vermin do not destroy and where thieves do not break in and steal. For where your treasure is, there your heart will be also.
MATTHEW 6:20 (NIV)

Business Meeting Notes

DATE: _____ / ____ / _____

_____
_____
_____
_____
_____
_____
_____
_____
_____
_____
_____
_____
_____
_____
_____
_____
_____
_____
_____
_____
_____
_____

Take Your Lessons to Heart

You've come a long way through this 90-day devotional. As you continue to read, let the principles and lessons from each entry establish in your head. Everything that gets discussed must be put into practice over and over. Today we speak on integrity, and dedication to God's word. God created and designed you to be great! He set a roadmap for you which can be found within His Word. Everything He gives you along the way should be used with integrity. Remain dedicated to following the Lord in good times and not so good.

We stand so much to gain with the Lord as our leader. We gain wisdom, understanding, knowledge, and discernment. He will give you the tools and resources to manage increase while simultaneously keeping you healthy mentally and physically. Any lapses in judgement leading you to act without integrity could cause you to miss out on the gifts God has for you. We have to be true with ourselves to avoid tricking ourselves into thinking things are better than they are in actuality. When you add too many cheat meals and justify it, you won't see ideal results in a fitness journey. We all know people who cheated in school and never fully grasped the subject(s) after taking shortcuts. The same can be said with everyday activities like customer interactions, family time, etc.

"He held fast to the Lord and did not stop following Him", taken from the scripture above which symbolizes dedication. We have to learn to see things through our spiritual eye. When we see things through a worldly eye, we open the door to be influenced by anyone that our faith is in vain. Following the Lord is no easy task but when it becomes more of a habit for you, it will feel like your natural way of doing business. Acting with integrity and dedication could propel and sustain our success making it easier to handle things you didn't think were possible on your own.

He held fast to the Lord and did not stop following Him; he kept the commands the Lord had given Moses. And the Lord was with Him; he was successful in whatever he undertook...
2 KINGS 18:6-7 (NIV)

Business Meeting Notes

DATE: _____ / / _____

_____
_____
_____
_____
_____
_____
_____
_____
_____
_____
_____
_____
_____
_____
_____
_____
_____
_____
_____
_____
_____
_____

Let Wisdom Be Your Guide

King Solomon's one true wish was for wisdom and God granted that him plus so much more. This shows us what happens when we make ourselves available for wisdom. It lays the foundation for all we seek in life and leads us to the blueprint of how to create our life's worth. King Solomon's request for wisdom solidified his place in history forever. He is credited with having written the book of proverbs and Ecclesiastes in the bible, in addition to the songs of Solomon.

In your quest for your promised land, place wisdom on your list for things to acquire. Get immersed into meaningful knowledge related to your calling. Learn from others who are doing similar works. Research and learn about their experiences. Learn about the customer base of the services being provided. Identify if there are any gaps in the information that you can fill with your own unique experiences.

Pray that God never stops grooming you in His word. Combining your acquisition of wisdom with what God can do spells generational prosperity. God can send you the right partnerships and other advantages to increase you in the midst of wisely working in your calling.

"So give your servant a discerning heart to govern your people and to distinguish between right and wrong. For who is able to govern this great people of yours?" The Lord was pleased that Solomon had asked for this. So God said to him, "Since you have asked for this and not for long life or wealth for yourself, nor have asked for the death of your enemies but for discernment in administering justice, I will do what you have asked. I will give you a wise and discerning heart, so that there will never have been anyone like you, nor will there ever be.
1 KINGS 3:9-12 (NIV)

Business Meeting Notes

DATE: ___/___/___

Trusting in You

Integrity is one of the biggest takeaways that people will have after being around you. God is the source of all good things and He is the source of your strength. You only have to accept it and not reject it. There are many reasons we need to understand how He shows up for us. Let's speak on integrity again.

Any lack of integrity in your life comes from a place of doubt. When you doubt your abilities you either seek help or seek shortcuts in order to advance. We have a tendency to fudge the truth when we aren't confident that we can achieve desired results. This commonly occurs when we are acting outside of the calling our Father wants us to follow. Any time we leave the Lord out of the equation, we place unnecessary pressure on ourselves and we can't be sure that things will work how we anticipate.

If we know that all things are possible through Christ, then we have no reason to doubt. With that said, integrity is an extension of our faith. When we believe in something and we are confident in the works of the Lord, we expect our reward and have no reason to doubt. When we act in accord with Him, much favor awaits us. God paves our way and causes everything around us to conform to His design. He will expose you to the public as a person of value and quality. People will easily recognize that they can place you in charge of their own valuables when they can trust you.

Whoever walks in integrity walks securely, but whoever takes crooked paths will be found out.
PROVERBS 10:9 (NIV)

And now, my daughter, don't be afraid. I will do for you all you ask. All the people of my town know that you are a woman of noble character.
RUTH 3:11 (NIV)

Business Meeting Notes

DATE: _____ / / _____

_____

_____

_____

_____

_____

_____

_____

_____

_____

_____

_____

_____

_____

_____

_____

_____

_____

_____

_____

_____

_____

_____

_____

Answer the Call Without Ceasing

Jesus was able to see above the distractions of the world. He understood that life on earth was only temporary but that His calling held a greater significance than the struggles of mortal life. He leaned on God and faced his calling head-on as we must do. How do we completely embrace the tasks God places on our hearts?

When He gives you a single task and you complete it, you gain a sense of accomplishment. The more you take on these individual tasks, you develop a habit of pleasing God which strengthens the overall relationship you have with Him. That habit is key! Growing your relationship with God is difficult in the beginning but the routine you develop will make pleasing the Lord a part of your day. Before you know it, you will feel out of place when you aren't answering the calling on your heart. When it becomes a lifestyle for you, as it was for Jesus, the "Peter" in your circle will not be able to tell you **NOT** to live your lifestyle, which consists of setting out to please God. You won't have a choice but to rebuke "Peter" when he suggests not handle your tasks assigned by God.

Your habits and your willingness to serve God opens the door for you to embrace those tasks. It generally takes us about two months to grow a habit. If you've read the previous entries every day, you have likely developed promising habits that will stick with you for some time. Keep it up! You'll naturally want to continue to actively serve God as you see your safety and well-being preserved for you. It makes you hungry for more and the servant relationship with God quickly turns into a friendship.

From that time on Jesus began to explain to His disciples that He must go to Jerusalem and suffer many things at the hands of the elders, the chief priests and the teachers of the law, and that He must be killed and on the third day be raised to life. Peter took Him aside and began to rebuke Him. "Never, Lord!" he said. "This shall never happen to you!" Jesus turned and said to Peter, "Get behind me, Satan! You are a stumbling block to me; you do not have in mind the concerns of God, but merely human concerns."
MATTHEW 16:21-23 (NIV)

Business Meeting Notes

DATE: _____ / / _____

He That Builds You Up

The devil always takes every opportunity to derail you but God strengthens you more and more each day. Along your journey, you will experience some setbacks which could feel unbearable. The feeling is temporary but the devil will try his best to turn that feeling into a lasting impression to take you away from your mission.

Because of your walk with God, you will be given the means and the strength to see face every challenge. Gradually, God does so much to build you up. With your faith, you can receive all that God is doing to build up your endurance. He seeks to make you stronger each time so that the challenge that derailed you yesterday cannot throw you off track today. Over time, you will find yourself in the middle of a challenge that would have caused you to give up in your past. Your new reaction however won't be to give up. Your new reaction will be the application of your faith and the tools you've received from God. He continues to work on you so that the challenge you'll meet in the future is easily overcome by applying all your training up that point.

A time will come when you look back at various challenges you faced in your life and will notice how far God has brought you. While the devil tries a variety of things to get your attention, God erects your fortification so high that you aren't affected in the same way you once were.

So if you think you are standing firm, be careful that you don't fall! No temptation has overtaken you except what is common to mankind. And God is faithful; He will not let you be tempted beyond what you can bear. But when you are tempted, He will also provide a way out so that you can endure it.
1 CORINTHIANS 10:12-14 (NIV)

Business Meeting Notes

DATE: _____ / / _____

Reminder to Shape Your Perspective

It is important not to feel defeated if things are different from what you planned. We've discussed how defeat is temporary and is used as a tool of the enemy. Though you may find yourself in a challenging situation, you never know what you will learn along the way. Our struggles present themselves for us to use them as lessons for growth. We have to change our perspective, because if we set our minds to learn, we can walk away with teachable lessons that will bring value to so many others for years to come.

We make it through tough times to come out better and more mature. In the midst of our struggles, we may meet some of the most amazing people and have experiences that permanently change our lives. Everything happens for a reason, so it's up to us to shine the right light on our situations. Remain hopeful, humble, and confident because the struggle is good for you and your soul.

And we know that in all things God works for the good of those who love Him, who have been called according to His purpose.
ROMANS 8:28 (NIV)

> OUR STRUGGLES PRESENT THEMSELVES FOR US TO USE THEM AS LESSONS FOR GROWTH.

Business Meeting Notes

DATE: _____ / / _____

_____
_____
_____
_____
_____
_____
_____
_____
_____
_____
_____
_____
_____
_____
_____
_____
_____
_____
_____
_____
_____
_____
_____
_____

Consuming Spirit

The scripture above depicts God's ability to work on our behalf as an independent force. He doesn't need any supplements for us to understand His power. He told the disciples that they won't need anything extra to help them on their journey—just the Holy Spirit! Remember a popular scripture that says seek ye first the kingdom and all else will be given unto you. Jesus says the same thing in another way in the text above. As long as you are serving the Lord, you will be blessed with all your necessities.

God's Spirit is powerful and you should fully invest in it with your soul, your body, and your mind. His Spirit should move us to the point that we speak His favor over our lives. It should move us so that we can speak healing over the lives of others who are suffering. His Spirit is more powerful than any schemes and traps of the devil. We must be fully invested in His Spirit because it will never fail us.

Read the following points over and over today to let it sink in:

- God's Spirit is the shift in the moment you need grace.
- His spirit is what delivers miracles and keeps us safe from destruction.
- God gives us the ability to decree things and they shall be. God gives us the power of healing.

When Jesus had called the Twelve together, He gave them power and authority to drive out all demons and to cure diseases, and He sent them out to proclaim the kingdom of God and to heal the sick. He told them: "Take nothing for the journey—no staff, no bag, no bread, no money, no extra shirt. Whatever house you enter, stay there until you leave that town. If people do not welcome you, leave their town and shake the dust off your feet as a testimony against them." So they set out and went from village to village, proclaiming the good news and healing people everywhere.
LUKE 9:1-6 (NIV)

Business Meeting Notes

DATE: _____ / / _____

_____

_____

_____

_____

_____

_____

_____

_____

_____

_____

_____

_____

_____

_____

_____

_____

_____

_____

_____

_____

_____

_____

_____

Practice Makes Perfect

Give God praise because He has amazing things in store for you! Your future gets clearer with every conversation that you have with Him. You have to find a way to confront God regularly so that you can gain from His presence. It is up to you to put yourself in a place where you are open to receive. Find a way to read the word, pray on the word, and practice the word all on a regular basis. Read, pray, and practice!

It will never be enough just to expose yourself to the word of the Lord. Blessed is the one that does what the word says! The bible says it's worse for a person who learns from the word and ignores it than someone who did not know any better from the start. Practice is the way forward and as you continue to go through this devotional, keep applying the past lessons along with the new lessons. Everything you see, read, and experience is for a reason. Remain vigilant in all God is asking of you because He leads you to toil on fertile ground. The success of your business depends on your willingness to consistently make God proud.

Blessed is the one who does not walk in step with the wicked or stand in the way that sinners take or sit in the company of mockers, but whose delight is in the law of the Lord, and who meditates on his law day and night. That person is like a tree planted by streams of water, which yields its fruit in season and whose leaf does not wither-- whatever they do prospers. Not so the wicked! They are like chaff that the wind blows away. Therefore the wicked will not stand in the judgment, nor sinners in the assembly of the righteous. For the Lord watches over the way of the righteous, but the way of the wicked leads to destruction.
PSALM 1:1-6 (NIV)

I keep my eyes always on the Lord. With Him at my right hand, I will not be shaken.
PSALM 16:8 (NIV)

Business Meeting Notes

DATE: _____ / _____ / _____

_____

_____

_____

_____

_____

_____

_____

_____

_____

_____

_____

_____

_____

_____

_____

_____

_____

_____

_____

_____

_____

_____

_____

_____

_____

_____

_____

Unpacking Visions

I n the scripture excerpt above, Daniel received an interpretation for a dream he had regarding four beasts. Upon receiving insight into the meaning of the complex dream, He became troubled as the vision represented despair. He believed the vision would impact Him somehow.

We focus on this excerpt today to cover the importance of sharing visions with others in order to get abstract ideas out of your head. Sometimes, we get messages and guidance from God that can be overwhelming. They are not always easy to understand which can be daunting, but verbalizing and explaining to someone else might lead to clarity.

As we grow in Him, we will have unique visions and prophecies. Do whatever it takes to reflect on the ideas and concepts that are imparted unto you. Sometimes this means allowing yourself to let your guard down and sharing your feelings with someone you trust. It helps to verbalize unclear encounters with God. Prophets throughout the bible received messages from God and shared the word for the sake of others as well as for their own sakes.

> *"This is the end of the matter. I, Daniel, was deeply troubled by my thoughts, and my face turned pale, but I kept the matter to myself."*
> DANIEL 7:28 (NIV)

DO WHATEVER IT TAKES TO REFLECT ON THE IDEAS AND CONCEPTS THAT ARE IMPARTED UNTO YOU.

Business Meeting Notes

DATE: _____ / / _____

Keep Anxiety Out

We've covered the topic of integrity multiple times and how it is an extension of faith. We discussed how doubt can affect your ability to act with integrity. Doubt usually comes when we're acting outside our calling. Anxiety is an extension of doubt and something that many people encounter. Anxiety can be mentally, physically, and spiritually harmful.

Like doubt, anxiety often occurs when you're outside your lane. Anxiety more so comes from timing factors, leading you to move before you should. We have to remind ourselves that we don't succeed in our own power. The glory, instead, belongs to the Lord. Similarly, God's timing is better than our timing and therefore we can't pressure ourselves to make things happen before the timing is right. You find yourself in a bind and beg God to clean up for you. When you anxiously press Him, your expectations usually fall short of what He is preparing for you. In that instance, you're asking God to re-write your life although He has already devised your path with perfection.

Be patient and steadfast in faith and prayer so that you are able to see and handle the gifts that He is preparing for you. God knows what will become of you and has known before you were created.

Good planning and hard work lead to prosperity, but hasty shortcuts lead to poverty.
PROVERBS 21:5 (NLT)

66

ANXIETY MORE SO COMES FROM TIMING
FACTORS, LEADING YOU TO MOVE
BEFORE YOU SHOULD.

99

Business Meeting Notes

DATE: _____ / / _____

_____

_____

_____

_____

_____

_____

_____

_____

_____

_____

_____

_____

_____

_____

_____

_____

_____

_____

_____

_____

_____

_____

Not Too Fast, But Not Too Slow

God's building process is crucial and surrendering to His timing is even more vital. Due to our nature, we want most things to happen instantaneously. However, what we have to realize is that the faster something happens, the less time we have to learn from it and understand it. When we expect something and remain expectant over a longer period of time, we actually soak it all in its fullness. The wait equips us with the tools to maintain when our expectations finally come to fruition.

We tend to develop a deeper appreciation for things that don't come to us overnight—in other words, things we have to work hard to obtain. It is easy for us to squander or mismanage anything we receive too quickly. When God takes His time to mold us into the people He wants us to be, He prepares us for the longer term. He won't delay anything from us to deny us. He is shaping us so that we can receive, sustain, and repeat the process with grace.

For the revelation awaits an appointed time; it speaks of the end and will not prove false. Though it linger, wait for it; it will certainly come and will not delay.
HABAKKUK 2:3 (NIV)

Those who work their land will have abundant food, but those who chase fantasies will have their fill of poverty.
PROVERBS 28:19–20 (NIV)

IT IS EASY FOR US TO SQUANDER OR MISMANAGE ANYTHING WE RECEIVE TOO QUICKLY.

Business Meeting Notes

DAY
75

DATE: _____/____/_____

_____

_____

_____

_____

_____

_____

_____

_____

_____

_____

_____

_____

_____

_____

_____

_____

_____

_____

_____

_____

_____

_____

_____

_____

_____

_____

_____

_____

Health Is Wealth

We speak about how the devil finds great joy when he's able to attack your body as you're approaching your promise land. Honor your body as a temple to the Lord by doing what you can to live a healthy life. Fight off the devil's tricks with improved eating habits and regular workout activity.

You can actually reach incredible heights in life but you can't enjoy the fruits of your labor if you're suffering from preventable chronic illness developed from poor health habits. It may not "feel" necessary now but you greatly decrease your chances of harboring disease in your body with regular exercise. As you focus on cleansing your soul and strengthening your mind, remember to be a complete person in health and works so that you don't miss the opportunities afforded to you. Be victorious over sickness by walking more, drinking more water, sleeping better, and eating vegetables daily. A good healthy glowing skin represents the goodness that God has for you in life.

Therefore, strengthen your feeble arms and weak knees. "Make level paths for your feet," so that the lame may not be disabled, but rather healed.
HEBREWS 12:12 (NIV)

> **HONOR YOUR BODY AS A TEMPLE TO THE LORD BY DOING WHAT YOU CAN TO LIVE A HEALTHY LIFE.**

Business Meeting Notes

DATE: _____ / / _____

_____
_____
_____
_____
_____
_____
_____
_____
_____
_____
_____
_____
_____
_____
_____
_____
_____
_____
_____
_____
_____
_____
_____
_____

A Calling Above Man

Your relationships will change over the course of time. Some relationships will break down if they weren't meant to be while others will become firm. When you make your dedicated walk with God, there are people you've known and grown with in life who will fade to the background. Some of them won't understand and others just won't mix in with what you're looking to do. It's possible you've experienced this during this 90-day devotional.

Vulnerability will set in at times as you completely shift to trust God with your life. During this period, take note of the types of people who emerge in your world. Some will seek to deter you but a certain few will seek to help build you up.

Be open to the changing relationships and pray for others who are on a similar path. Pray for them to maintain the struggle just as you would want someone to support and pray for you. You might find change uncomfortable but a lot can be gained when you're out of your comfort zone. Embrace the change and continue to be faithful.

Then Jesus said to His disciples, "Whoever wants to be my disciple must deny themselves and take up their cross and follow me. For whoever wants to save their life will lose it, but whoever loses their life for me will find it. What good will it be for someone to gain the whole world, yet forfeit their soul? Or what can anyone give in exchange for their soul?
MATTHEW 16:24–26 (NIV)

Whoever will not carry the cross that is given to them when they follow me cannot be my follower.
LUKE 14:27 (NIV)

Business Meeting Notes

DATE: _____ / / _____

_____
_____
_____
_____
_____
_____
_____
_____
_____
_____
_____
_____
_____
_____
_____
_____
_____
_____
_____
_____
_____
_____
_____
_____
_____

Confidence in Your Calling

Allow God to build you up so that you are confident in who He called you to be. If you leave the door open for doubting yourself, the devil will send opposition to lie to you in an attempt to deter you from who you were called to be. A lot of your confidence will come from your faith that God can answer all your calls and do exceedingly abundant things for you. With that knowledge in our back pocket, you see through falsehood when the devil's workers speak poorly of you. People with good intentions can encourage you in ways you didn't know you needed. Depending on the situation we can also receive confirmation and a refined understanding of our mission based on conversations with friends and foes.

"Have I not commanded you? Be strong and courageous! Do not tremble or be dismayed, for the Lord your God is with you wherever you go."
JOSHUA 1:9 (NASB)

If the Lord is pleased with us, then He will bring us into this land and give it to us – a land which flows with milk and honey. "Only do not rebel against the Lord; and do not fear the people of the land, for they will be our prey. Their protection has been removed from them, and the Lord is with us; do not fear them."
NUMBERS 14:8–9 (NASB)

> A LOT OF YOUR CONFIDENCE WILL COME FROM YOUR FAITH THAT GOD CAN ANSWER ALL YOUR CALLS AND DO EXCEEDINGLY ABUNDANT THINGS FOR YOU.

Business Meeting Notes

DAY
78

DATE: ___/___/___

_____
_____
_____
_____
_____
_____
_____
_____
_____
_____
_____
_____
_____
_____
_____
_____
_____
_____
_____
_____
_____
_____
_____
_____

What Will They Call You?

We have a long road to travel before we fully realize our destiny. Along the way, God will place courage and grace within us. Over the course of time, we will transform and our evolution will not cease. This transformation will benefit us, and those around us throughout the journey. The prophet Isaiah speaks the word of the Lord saying that He will take delight in you.

God gives you a design for your life. He is willing to reveal many secrets with us. Through His guidance we get insight on who we are destined to be. When we get visions of the outline for our lives and then compare it to our actual lives, we usually see a gap. However, everyday is an opportunity to pray and work to close that gap. Assess your current habits and find what you could do differently.

The crown of favor we receive is a rewarding adornment for our work and diligence in the Lord. When it is all said and done, you will be called great and amazing by many!

After Jacob returned from Paddan Aram, God appeared to him again and blessed him. God said to him, "Your name is Jacob, but you will no longer be called Jacob; your name will be Israel." So He named him Israel. And God said to him, "I am God Almighty; be fruitful and increase in number. A nation and a community of nations will come from you, and kings will be among your descendants. The land I gave to Abraham and Isaac I also give to you, and I will give this land to your descendants after you." Then God went up from him at the place where He had talked with him.
GENESIS 35:9–15 (NIV)

The nations will see your vindication, and all kings your glory; you will be called by a new name that the mouth of the Lord will bestow. You will be a crown of splendor in the Lord's hand, a royal diadem in the hand of your God. No longer will they call you Deserted, or name your land Desolate. But you will be called Hephzibah, and your land Beulah; for the Lord will take delight in you, and your land will be married.
ISAIAH 62:2–4 (NIV)

DATE: _____/____/_____

_____

_____

_____

_____

_____

_____

_____

_____

_____

_____

_____

_____

_____

_____

_____

_____

_____

_____

_____

_____

_____

_____

_____

_____

_____

Hallelujah

From the beginning, God wanted us to trust Him in the Garden of Eden. He led Israel out of Egypt through the middle of a sea. He turned stones to bread and provided water in the desert and wilderness. He sent angels to fight battles and win wars for the kings that he established. He impregnated a virgin with His own Son who would die for our sins and transgressions to be forgiven.

No matter what goes on in life, take comfort in the fact that God is unchanging. Take comfort in the fact that He knows everything that will happen and when it will happen. He continues to work in our lives consistently every day. Who we are today is nothing like who we were last year. He gave us another new day, equipped with a sound mind and security for us to keep pushing. There is nothing that He hasn't given us because the victory in the battles we have yet to face are already won!

God is everlasting and unchanging. He has been around long before we could remember and He will be around long after we pass away. As our creator, He is and always will be the most constant thing that we know. His grace allows us to develop into the people He wants us to be. We can always call on His name and be sure that He will be available for us. He wants us to rely on Him for daily coverage and provisions.

But thanks be to God! He gave us the victory through our Lord Jesus Christ. Therefore, my dear brothers and sisters, stand firm. Let nothing move you. Always give yourselves fully to the work of the Lord, because you know that your labor in the Lord is not in vain.
1 CORINTHIANS 15:57 (NIV)

Be strong and courageous. Do not be afraid or terrified because of them, for the Lord your God goes with you; He will never leave you nor forsake you."
DEUTERONOMY 31:6 (NIV)

Have mercy on me, my God, have mercy on me, for in you I take refuge. I will take refuge in the shadow of your wings until the disaster has passed.
PSALM 59:1 (NIV)

Business Meeting Notes

DATE: _____ / / _____

_____

_____

_____

_____

_____

_____

_____

_____

_____

_____

_____

_____

_____

_____

_____

_____

_____

_____

_____

_____

_____

_____

_____

Faith in the Unseen

Even as we are this far into the 90 days, we have to stick to the basics. We have been introduced to the tools and we have to continue to use them so not to lose them. It may appear that our thinking gets repetitive but we are operating under one leader with a set of uniform requirements. One of those is our faith, which is a baseline component of our existence. Faith keeps us connected to the privileges found in the Lord whenever we want to give up. Let's look at how this happens...

When we do things based on perception alone, we hinder God's ability to have control in our lives. If we make decisions based on our current situation or surroundings, we put our journey at risk by possibly opening the door to doubt and anxiety. Before David became king of Israel, he was a shepherd. Imagine the perception when Goliath, a giant and known warrior, charged David only to meet his own demise. David established a profound reputation when he slayed Goliath and this was all because of his faith in the Lord.

In another biblical story, Noah heard from God that a flood would wipe away the inhabitants of the earth, although a rain storm of that magnitude was something that had never happened before. Because of Noah's faith in God, he built an ark and gathered his family to lead them to their salvation through the 40 days and 40 nights of storms.

With faith, we open ourselves up for all the hard-to-imagine possibilities that come with God's planning. It's fine if our own plan does not go according to its outline. God's way is always greater and there is no true comparison. Let the lures and the opinions from the world fade to your background and allow His design to influence your habits, your schedule, your lifestyle, and your focus.

For we walk by faith, not by sight.
2 CORINTHIANS 5:7 (NKJV)

The Philistine said to David, "Come to me, and I will give your flesh to the birds of the air and to the beasts of the field." Then David said to the Philistine, "You come to me with a sword and with a spear and with a javelin, but I come to you in the name of the Lord of hosts, the God of armies of Israel, whom you have defied. This day the Lord will deliver you into my hand, and I will strike you down and cut off your head."
1 SAMUEL 17:44–46 (ESV)

Business Meeting Notes

DATE: _____ / / _____

_____
_____
_____
_____
_____
_____
_____
_____
_____
_____
_____
_____
_____
_____
_____
_____
_____
_____
_____
_____
_____
_____
_____
_____

Eat to Live

The devil seeks to derail your strides to get closer to God and he will try anything to confuse your senses. He will lead you to buy something you don't need just so that he can later break that which you purchased. The devil will be proud if such a sequence of events then leads you to have buyer's remorse. The devil can play on your senses in other ways and will make you feel like time is running out on a project you're working on. If he causes you to fear, you may rush anxiously without checking the quality of your work. The devil appreciates it when he can make you work below standard. He likes it more when you kick yourself about such an outcome.

The devil will do things with the hopes of making you cry and unsettled. This is why we must be victorious over worldly things and ideas which can turn into the devil's playground. Our focus should be on heavenly things which is where our real gifts originate. Maintain excitement for God's promises which are truly out of this world. You will surely overcome the attacks.

Then Jesus was led by the Spirit into the wilderness to be tempted there by the devil. For forty days and forty nights He fasted and became very hungry. During that time the devil came and said to Him, "If you are the Son of God, tell these stones to become loaves of bread." But Jesus told Him, "No! The Scriptures say, 'People do not live by bread alone, but by every word that comes from the mouth of God."
MATTHEW 4:1-4 (NLT)

66

OUR FOCUS SHOULD BE ON HEAVENLY THINGS WHICH IS WHERE OUR REAL GIFTS ORIGINATE.

99

Business Meeting Notes

DATE: _____ / / _____

_____
_____
_____
_____
_____
_____
_____
_____
_____
_____
_____
_____
_____
_____
_____
_____
_____
_____
_____
_____
_____
_____

Like Music for the Soul

Take pride in the fact that God calls on you. Not everyone can hear a clear message from God even though we are His creation. The book of James describes others who can hear the message but are not able to apply it. They receive the tools, yet lose them because they are not put to use. But not you, for you are good soil for the word that is planted in you. Consider it joy when you receive and decipher what God speaks to you.

God's purpose will cause us to be fulfilled in everything we do. His purpose will cause us to be overflowing with fruit that will have a positive effect on the people who are around. It does not always put you in a comfort zone but be grateful that you hear His calling for it will stretch your territory. Though you may experience growing pains, you should be delighted that you can sense God working in your heart.

Rejoice and praise God for His love and kindness. Praise Him for the way you are wonderfully made in His likeness. With Him there is never a lasting sorrow.

He replied, "Blessed rather are those who hear the Word of God and obey it."
LUKE 11:28 (NIV)

66

CONSIDER IT JOY WHEN YOU RECEIVE AND DECIPHER WHAT GOD SPEAKS TO YOU.

99

Business Meeting Notes

DATE: _____ / / _____

Fruit from the Tree of Fulfillment

The fruit of the spirit is a measurement on your level of fulfillment. If you have love in your life, then it means you have joy, which means there is peace, and room for patience. When you consider the fruit, you notice that everything goes hand-in-hand. If anything is missing, you must evaluate why you're experiencing some without the others and pray for answers. Take time to reflect on each item of the spiritual fruit in your daily journey.

You'll know that you are living a purpose-driven life when you experience all aspects from love through self-control and nothing is absent. You should also experience these in any meaningful relationships you share with others. Reflecting on them is a good way to assess the status of these relationships.

But the fruit of the Spirit is love, joy, peace, patience, kindness, goodness, faithfulness, gentleness, self-control; against such things there is no law. And those who belong to Christ Jesus have crucified the flesh with its passions and desires. If we live by the Spirit, let us also keep in step with the Spirit. Let us not become conceited, provoking one another, envying one another.
GALATIANS 5:22–26 (ESV)

But you, man of God, flee from all this, and pursue righteousness, godliness, faith, love, endurance and gentleness. Fight the good fight of the faith. Take hold of the eternal life to which you were called when you made your good confession in the presence of many witnesses.
1 TIMOTHY 6:11–12 (NIV)

TAKE TIME TO REFLECT ON EACH ITEM OF THE SPIRITUAL FRUIT IN YOUR DAILY JOURNEY.

Business Meeting Notes

DATE: _____ / / _____

The Gift of Ability

God wants to place us in prosperous and fertile territory surrounded by abundance. He will do amazing things for us, and He will never leave us stranded. It is up to us to continue studying under Him as His will is done. God wants us to be whole and complete in spirit and mind so that we can fully enjoy His promises. He wants us to be sound individuals who can utilize our gifts to lead others toward Him.

As long as we maintain the perspective that He is for us, then we are capable of achieving our wildest dreams. Go to Him in prayer and work on developing your gifts. Develop your perseverance to push through when early results don't match your efforts. His word encourages us to be committed to running the race of endurance instead of speed. No matter what happens, He reassures us that He doesn't guide us to let us down. Through it all, find meaning in the midst of your progress to learn how to consistently thrive in all you do. It is our duty to acknowledge that He is the driving force behind all our success and as long as we rely on Him, He will build us with mental and physical capabilities to manage greatness.

I can do all things through Christ who strengthens me.
PHILIPPIANS 4:13 (NKJV)

> ## HE WANTS US TO BE SOUND INDIVIDUALS WHO CAN UTILIZE OUR GIFTS TO LEAD OTHERS TOWARD HIM.

Business Meeting Notes

DATE: _____ / _____ / _____

_____

_____

_____

_____

_____

_____

_____

_____

_____

_____

_____

_____

_____

_____

_____

_____

_____

_____

_____

_____

_____

_____

All Things New

Embrace the entrepreneur you're becoming as you walk with God. The Bible says His word is a lamp to guide my feet and a light for my path *(Psalm 119:105)*. Through your commitment to seek Him daily on behalf of your business, you'll begin to see changes in how you perform and in the ways you show up in your business. You'll start to see a rise in peace, while the anxiety of making the next sale will fade away.

There will be times that you won't recognize yourself because of how you react. You might look different now compared to old pictures captured when you were going through a rough phase. God works in you and does a new thing in you. You will transform and you will notice changes over time. Embrace the new you and accept the goodness that will shine through you. Be open and graceful yet make sure you are observant and discerning so that you don't stumble.

But to all who believed Him and accepted Him, He gave the right to become children of God. They are reborn—not with a physical birth resulting from human passion or plan, but a birth that comes from God.
JOHN 1:12-13 (NLT)

> EMBRACE THE NEW YOU AND ACCEPT
> THE GOODNESS THAT WILL SHINE
> THROUGH YOU.

Business Meeting Notes

DATE: _____/____/_____

Fasting God's Way

Your business is a ministry that forms a relationship where you are responsible for improving the lives of your constituents. It is your arena to pass on all the favor God has given to you through your talents. Although you are a go-to expert, integrity and humility should spill over from your interactions with your customers. In other words God's grace should shine through you and your company.

When you fast God's way, you align yourself with the ways of the Lord. The Lord is kind and loving in nature. We on the other hand are naturally influenced by the ways of this world which lead us to be short-tempered and hasty. Fasting can bring us back to empathizing with our customers challenges. The fasting He wants us to do causes us to reset our thinking. Fasting could lead to new strategies to better serve. God will also reveal where we have been wasteful or unproductive and will show us a new path. Maybe all answers won't be given to you in a single day, but there is no limit to how often you can fast as long as you do it with the intentions of aligning your spirit, and the spirit of your business with God's love.

"Shout! A full-throated shout! Hold nothing back—a trumpet-blast shout! Tell my people what's wrong with their lives, face my family Jacob with their sins! They're busy, busy, busy at worship, and love studying all about me. To all appearances they're a nation of right-living people— law-abiding, God-honoring. They ask me, 'What's the right thing to do?' and love having me on their side. But they also complain, 'Why do we fast and you don't look our way? Why do we humble ourselves and you don't even notice?' "Well, here's why: "The bottom line on your 'fast days' is profit. You drive your employees much too hard. You fast, but at the same time you bicker and fight. You fast, but you swing a mean fist. The kind of fasting you do won't get your prayers off the ground. Do you think this is the kind of fast day I'm after: a day to show off humility? To put on a pious long face and parade around solemnly in black? Do you call that fasting, a fast day that I, God, would like? "This is the kind of fast day I'm after: to break the chains of injustice, get rid of exploitation in the workplace, free the oppressed, cancel debts. What I'm interested in seeing you do is: sharing your food with the hungry, inviting the homeless poor into your homes, putting clothes on the shivering ill-clad, being available to your own families. Do this and the lights will turn on, and your lives will turn around at once. Your righteousness will pave your way. The God of glory will secure your passage. Then when you pray, God will answer. You'll call out for help and I'll say, 'Here I am.'
ISAIAH 58:1-9 MSG

Business Meeting Notes

DAY
87

DATE: _____ / / _____

_____

_____

_____

_____

_____

_____

_____

_____

_____

_____

_____

_____

_____

_____

_____

_____

_____

_____

_____

_____

_____

_____

_____

_____

_____

_____

Preparation Mindset

As an entrepreneur, you're going to experience peaks and valleys in your business. The key to prospering even in the valley is preparation. Seek the Lord for wisdom on how to govern your resources. The goal is to save in seasons of high revenue so that you stabilize during those slow periods.

In the book of Genesis, God teaches us that we must always be in preparation mode. We never know what is in store for us tomorrow, so we must have a preparation mindset today. Joseph found himself in a flourishing Egypt during a time when famine was on the horizon. He wisely instructed Pharaoh to store the abundance that Egypt had been blessed with. When famine eventually came, Egypt was able to provide for neighboring territories who were on the brink of death.

When you come into favor in your business, no matter the shape or form, be a good steward. God provides for us on purpose. Part of our purpose is to act with wisdom and understanding that God intends for us to use our resources with self-control which is part of the fruit of the spirit. There is a time and place for everything, including saving and spending. Avoid the trap of squandering your money in the wrong places which is usually facilitated by worldly attractions. Read Genesis 41 today and seek God on how you can better prepare today for times to come.

Let Pharaoh appoint commissioners over the land to take a fifth of the harvest of Egypt during the seven years of abundance. They should collect all the food of these good years that are coming and store up the grain under the authority of Pharaoh, to be kept in the cities for food. This should be held in reserve for the country to be used during the seven years of famine that will come upon Egypt, so that the country may not be ruined by the famine.
GENESIS 41:34–36 (NIV)

"Bring the whole tithe into the storehouse, that there may be food in my house. Test me in this," says the Lord Almighty, "and see if I will not throw open the floodgates of heaven and pour out so much blessing that there will not be room enough to store it. I will prevent pests from devouring your crops, and the vines in your fields will not drop their fruit before it is ripe," says the Lord Almighty. "Then all the nations will call you blessed, for yours will be a delightful land," says the Lord Almighty.
MALACHI 3:10–12 (NIV)

Business Meeting Notes

DATE: _____ / / _____

_____
_____
_____
_____
_____
_____
_____
_____
_____
_____
_____
_____
_____
_____
_____
_____
_____
_____
_____
_____
_____

Assets > Liabilities

D o you find yourself with never-ending bills? Your mind has to shift to the wealthy person that you are. You have to visualize your true self and not see a consumer that the world has trained us to be. Deep down inside you are a wealthy person but you have to create a plan to save your wealth. Even when it doesn't seem like it to you, God is your wealth and you are blessed and wealthy because you are a child of God. God will not forsake His people. However, He wants you to be trained and disciplined in doing what is right.

Start small by building an actual savings that is substantial. Savings will take place when you live below your means. Instead of managing your money by investing in perishables to impress others, consider if you can go another day without making the purchase. Then see if you can last another day, and another. Your mission is not to look wealthy, but to actually become wealthy. Wealth does not have a look but it shows as an abundance of resources with actual value – not a large price tag. It could be real estate properties, franchises, multiple successful companies, etc.

Tithing will help you on your journey. It depletes your earnings by 10%, leaving you with enough to obtain what you need. Over time, you get better at living below your means and realize how much you have leftover for savings, even after tithing. Move away from buying things to impress others and work toward the joy you get by impressing God through obedience. We can't expect God to give us more, when we haven't been proper stewards over what we have currently.

But remember the Lord your God, for it is He who gives you the ability to produce wealth, and so confirms His covenant, which He swore to your ancestors, as it is today.
DEUTERONOMY 8:18 (NIV)

"His master replied, 'Well done, good and faithful servant! You have been faithful with a few things; I will put you in charge of many things. Come and share your master's happiness!'
MATTHEW 25:21 (NIV)

Honor the Lord with your wealth, with the firstfruits of all your crops; then your barns will be filled to overflowing, and your vats will brim over with new wine.
PROVERBS 3:9 (NIV)

The wise have wealth and luxury, but fools spend whatever they get.
PROVERBS 21:20 (NLT)

Business Meeting Notes

DATE: _____ / / _____

_____
_____
_____
_____
_____
_____
_____
_____
_____
_____
_____
_____
_____
_____
_____
_____
_____
_____
_____

New Beginnings

Congratulations! You have made it to the end of this 90-day journey with God. 90-days of seeking Him on behalf of your business. I pray that you can see now that God is leading you toward growth and expansion. In the book of Genesis, He tells us to be fruitful and multiply. Expanded responsibility will come with expanded territory. It remains your responsibility to attain the wisdom to facilitate that growth.

Ask yourself "what knowledge will assist you on your overall journey?" When you face challenges with growing pains, ask yourself "where are the specific sources of the challenges?" Asking yourself questions directly tied to growth pains will lead you to the best solutions to keep you going. Never stop asking God for guidance as He will give you the confidence needed to execute each day.

Be intentional, and do whatever you can to feed God's will in your life. Take the initiative to soak in His word. You have people that pray for you, yet your own faith in the Lord and your own effort allows you to conquer everything that comes with growth. Maintain your courage throughout your life so that you don't succumb to pressures that fall in your lap as a result of your growth. Face it head-on because with God, anything is possible, no matter the magnitude.

BE INTENTIONAL, AND DO WHATEVER YOU
CAN TO FEED GOD'S WILL IN YOUR LIFE.

Business Meeting Notes

DATE: _____ / / _____

_____

_____

_____

_____

_____

_____

_____

_____

_____

_____

_____

_____

_____

_____

_____

_____

_____

_____

_____

_____

_____

_____

_____

_____

Author Bio

TATUM TEMIA AYOMIKE is an award-winning entrepreneur, executive producer, author and devoted Christian who has committed her life to helping women bridge the gap between faith and business. Her impact as the CEO of Anchored Media includes a global reach of millions of listeners across 75+ produced podcast shows in just 2 years. Through her personal brand, Tatum has cultivated a community of businesswomen who give God full authority to use their business as a vessel for the Kingdom. Using the word of God as her platform, Tatum's prayer journal and published books offer instrumental guidance to 'boss up' in any entrepreneurial venture. Tatum has been featured in several magazines and publications and has been named as a Top 30 under 30 in the Washington, DC area.

Learn more at www.tatumtemia.com and follow on Instagram:
@tatumtemia & @blessedandbossedup

Made in the USA
Las Vegas, NV
20 March 2024

87457991R00105